Everyman, I will go with thee,
and be thy guide

THE EVERYMAN
LIBRARY

*The Everyman Library was founded by J. M. Dent
in 1906. He chose the name Everyman because he wanted
to make available the best books ever written in every
field to the greatest number of people at the cheapest possible
price. He began with Boswell's 'Life of Johnson';
his one-thousandth title was Aristotle's 'Metaphysics',
by which time sales exceeded forty million.*

*Today Everyman paperbacks remain true to
J. M. Dent's aims and high standards, with a wide range
of titles at affordable prices in editions which address
the needs of today's readers. Each new text is reset to give
a clear, elegant page and to incorporate the latest thinking
and scholarship. Each book carries the pilgrim logo,
the character in 'Everyman', a medieval mystery play,
a proud link between Everyman
past and present.*

AMOROUS RITES

ELIZABETHAN
EROTIC NARRATIVE VERSE

Edited by
SANDRA CLARK
Birkbeck College, London

EVERYMAN
J. M. DENT · LONDON
CHARLES E. TUTTLE
VERMONT

Introduction and other critical material © J. M. Dent, 1994

All rights reserved

First published in Everyman in 1994

J. M. Dent
Orion Publishing Group
Orion House
5 Upper St Martin's Lane
London WC2H 9EA
and
Charles E. Tuttle Co. Inc.
28 South Main Street
Rutland, Vermont 05701, USA

Typeset in Sabon by CentraCet Limited, Cambridge
Printed in Great Britain by
The Guernsey Press Co. Ltd, Guernsey, C. I.

This book if bound as a paperback is subject to
the condition that it may not be issued on loan or otherwise
except in its original binding.

British Library Cataloguing-in-Publication Data
is available upon request.

ISBN 0 460 87530 2

CONTENTS

NOTE ON THE EDITOR

SANDRA CLARK has published books and articles on Elizabethan and Jacobean literature, particularly popular prose and drama, and Shakespeare. Her most recent publication is *The Plays of Beaumont and Fletcher: Sexual Themes and Dramatic Representation* (Hemel Hempstead, 1994). The idea for the anthology which has become *Amorous Rites* originated in a seminar at Birkbeck College, University of London, where problems arose from the lack of easily available texts.

Year	Age	Life
?1558		Birth of Thomas Lodge, second son of a prosperous grocer, Sir Thomas Lodge, later Lord Mayor of London
1564		Birth of Christopher Marlowe, second of nine children of John Marlowe, a shoemaker, at Canterbury Birth of William Shakespeare, eldest son of John Shakespeare, a tradesman, and Mary, née Arden
1571	13	Lodges enters Merchant Taylors School
1573	15	Lodge enters Trinity College, Oxford, as a scholar

(N.B. no attempt is made to assign dates to all of Shakespeare's plays)

CHRONOLOGY OF THEIR TIMES

Year	Artistic Events	Historical Events
1558		Accession of Elizabeth I, crowned the following year Re-establishment of Protestantism
1559	Publication of the Elizabethan *Book of Common Prayer*	Peace between England and France
1560	Publication of the anonymous *Fable of Ovid treting of Narcissus*	
1561	Birth of Francis Bacon Hoby's translation of Castiglione's *The Courtier*	
1563		First Elizabethan Poor Law
1564	Death of Michelangelo	Birth of Galileo; Death of Calvin
1565	Publication of Golding's translation of Ovid's *Metamorphoses*, Books 1–4, dedicated to the Earl of Leicester; the remaining books published in 1567 Peend's *Hermaphroditus and Salmacis*	
1566		Birth of the future James I
1570		The Pope excommunicates and deposes Elizabeth I
1571		Battle of Lepanto
1572	Birth of John Donne and Ben Jonson Act of Parliament passed declaring unpatronised troupes of actors to be rogues and vagabonds	St Bartholomew Day massacre of Protestants in Paris

Year	Age	Life
1576		Birth of John Marston, son of John Marston, a lawyer of Coventry
1577	19	Lodge receives BA degree
1578	20	Lodge enters Lincoln's Inn, but does not continue long in the study of law
1579	15	Marlowe enters as a scholar at the King's School, Canterbury
1580	16	Marlowe enters Corpus Christi College, Cambridge, on a scholarship endowed by Archbishop Parker. While studying at Cambridge, he meets, among others, Thomas Nashe
	22	Lodge publishes *The Defence of Poetry, Music, and Stage Plays* in answer to Stephen Gosson's *The School of Abuse* (1579)
1582	18	Shakespeare marries Anne Hathaway
1583	19	Birth of Susanna Shakespeare
	25	By this year Lodge has a wife, Joan, and a daughter, Mary
1584	26	Lodge publishes *An Alarum against Usurers*; he goes on a voyage with Captain Clark to the Canaries and the Azores until 1589
	20	Marlowe receives BA; around this time, he may have begun to work as a government spy
1584–5		Birth of Francis Beaumont at Grace-Dieu, Leicestershire, third son of Francis Beaumont, a Justice of the Common Pleas. Both his parents and some cousins on his mother's side were at various times in trouble for assisting the Catholic cause
1585	21	Birth of Hamnet and Judith Shakespeare, twins; Hamnet dies in 1596. Shakespeare may have left Stratford around this time
	21	Portrait of Marlowe, now hanging in Corpus Christi College, painted

Year	Artistic Events	Historical Events
1576	Erection of the Theatre, probably the first purpose-built theatre in England, in Finsbury	
1577	Opening of the Curtain theatre and the Blackfriars theatre	First edition of Holinshed's *Chronicles of England, Scotland, and Ireland* Drake begins his voyage round the world, completed 1580
1578	Lyly, *Euphues, or the anatomy of Wit*	
1579	Spenser, *The Shepheardes Calendar*, published anonymously North's translation of Plutarch's *Lives of the Noble Grecians and Romans*	Discussions of possible marriage between Elizabeth I and Alençon, Duke of Anjou
1580	Montaigne, *Essais* Stow, *The Chronicles of England*, subsequently called *Annales* Lyly, *Euphues his England*	
1583	Stanyhurst's translation of *Aeneid*, Books 1–4	
1584		Failure of Raleigh's expedition in Virginia

Year	Age	Life
1586	22	Marlowe may have written *Dido, Queen of Carthage*, with Nashe
1587	23	Around this time, Shakespeare possibly joins the Queen's Men as an actor
	23	Marlowe receives MA, after intervention of the Privy Council on his behalf, despite rumours tht he had joined the Catholic seminary at Rheims. *Tamburlaine the Great* being performed during the summer
1589	25	Marlowe imprisoned in Newgate after a street fight
	31	*Scylla's Metamorphosis*, by Lodge, published in a volume of poems including sonnets and a satire
1589–90	25–6	Shakespeare probably starts to write plays; early works include the *Henry VI* plays, *The Taming of the Shrew*, *The Comedy of Errors*, *Titus Andronicus*
1590	32	Lodge publishes *Rosalynde*, a prose romance later used by Shakespeare as the basis for *As You Like It*
	26	Marlowe's *Tamburlaine the Great* (both parts) published anonymously; he possibly wrote *The Massacre at Paris* and *The Jew of Malta* around this time
1591	15	Marston enters Brasenose College, Oxford
	27	Marlowe sharing lodgings with Thomas Kyd, the playwright, at this time
	33	Lodge publishes *The Famous, True and Historical Life of Robert, second Duke of Normandy*, and *Catharos. Diogenes in his Singularitie*; he sails with Thomas Cavendish on an ill-fated voyage to South America
1592	28	Robert Greene calls Shakespeare 'an upstart crow' (*Greene's Groatsworth of Wit*)
	28	Marlowe summoned on a charge of assault; fights a (non-fatal) duel in Canterbury; attacked by Robert Greene in *Greenes Groatsworth of Wit* for 'diabolical atheism'; he may have written *Edward II* this year
1593	29	Kyd is arrested and heretical papers which he attributes to Marlowe are found in their room; Marlowe is summoned to appear before the Privy Council on a charge of heresy, and is killed by Ingram Frizer at Deptford while on bail, May 30; Frizer is subsequently pardoned

Year	Artistic Events	Historical Events
1586	Decree of the Star Chamber that all published works must first receive ecclesiastical approval Death of Sidney	Battle of Zutphen
1587		Execution of Mary, Queen of Scots
1588	Harriot, *A brief and true report of the new found land of Virginia*	Defeat of the Spanish Armada
1589	Puttenham, *The Art of English Poetry* Hakluyt, *The Principal Navigations, Voyages, Traffics . . .*	
1590	Spenser, *The Faerie Queene*, Books 1–3 Sidney, *The Countess of Pembroke's Arcadia* (further editions in 1593 and 1598)	
1591	Sidney, *Astrophel and Stella* Harington, translation of Ariosto's *Orlando Furioso*	
1592	Death of Robert Greene	Severe outbreak of plague in London, causing the closure of the theatres for three months
1593	Birth of George Herbert	Plague again rife in London, theatres closed for considerable periods of time

Year	Age	Life
1593	29	Shakespeare publishes *Venus and Adonis*, dedicated to the Earl of Southampton
	35	Lodge returns to England; he publishes *The Life and Death of William Longbeard*, and *Phillis*, a sonnet sequence
1594		Marlowe's *Edward II* and *Dido, Queen of Carthage* published posthumously
	10	Beaumont matriculates at Broadgates Hall, Oxford
	36	Lodge publishes *Euphues Shadow* and *The Wounds of Civil War*, a play based on Plutarch
	30	Shakespeare publishes *The Rape of Lucrece*, also dedicated to Southampton; he becomes a member of the Lord Chamberlain's Men
	18	Marston receives BA and either this year or the next begins residence at the Middle Temple, where he shares rooms with his father until the latter's death in 1599
1595		Marlowe's translation, *All Ovid's Elegies*, published posthumously
	31	Shakespeare probably writes *A Midsummer Night's Dream*, *Romeo and Juliet*
	37	Lodge publishes *A Fig for Momus*, a collection of satirical poetry
1596	32	John Shakespeare applies for a coat of arms; William Shakespeare lodging in Bankside at this time
	38	Lodge publishes three pamphlets, *The Divel Conjured*, the romance *A Margarite of America*, composed while in South America, and *Wit's Misery and the World's Madness*. He leaves England around this time on account of either religious or financial difficulties, and he studies medicine in Avignon. By this time his first wife had died and he was married to Jane Albridge (or Aldred), a widow and a Catholic
1597	33	Shakespeare buys New Place, Stratford
1598	34	Shakespeare acts in Ben Jonson's *Everyman in his Humour* Marlowe's *Hero and Leander* published posthumously
	22	Marston publishes *The Metamorphosis of Pygmalion's Image and Certain Satires*, followed soon after by a collection of satires, *The Scourge of Villainy*

Year	Artistic Events	Historical Events
1594		Beginning of a period of bad harvests in England; plague in London until summer
1595	Sidney, *The Defence of Poesy* Chapman, *Ovid's Banquet of Sense* Drayton, *Endimion and Phoebe: Idea's Latmus*	Raleigh's voyage to Guiana Unsuccessful voyage of Drake and Hawkins to the West Indies and deaths of both
1596	Spenser, *The Faerie Queene*, Books 1–6	Expedition of Essex to Cadiz
1597	First version of Bacon's *Essays* (further editions, 1612, 1625) James I, *Daemonologie*	Failure of the second Spanish Armada because of bad weather
1598	Chapman's translation of Homer's *Iliad*, Books 1–7 Meres, *Palladis Tamia* Jonson, *Everyman in his Humour* Stow, *A Survay of London*	

Year	Age	Life
1598	40	Lodge qualifies as a doctor and returns to England; he practices medicine mainly among Catholic recusants in London and publishes *A Looking Glass for London and England*, a play written in collaboration with Robert Greene, which appeared on the London stage in 1592
1598–9	22–3	Marston's involvement in the War of the Theatres and writing of *Histriomastix*, which satirises Ben Jonson
1599	33	Further editions of Marston's *The Scourge of Villainy* ordered to be burnt by the Bishop of London and the Archbishop of Canterbury
	35	Shakespeare praised for his plays by Francis Meres in *Palladis Tamia*; works mentioned by name are *The Two Gentlemen of Verona, The Comedy of Errors, Love's Labours Lost* (also '*Love's Labour's Won*'), *A Midsummer Night's Dream, The Merchant of Venice, Richard II, Richard III, Henry VI, King John, Titus Andronicus, Romeo and Juliet*, and 'his sugred sonnets among his private friends'; he writes *Henry V* this year
1600	36	Around this time Shakespeare writes *As You Like It, Twelfth Night, Hamlet*
	16	Beaumont enters Inner Temple. Probably formed friendships with Ben Jonson and perhaps John Marston around this time
		Lucan's First Book Translated Line for Line, by Marlowe, published posthumously
	34	Marston writes *Jack Drum's Entertainment*, put on by the Children of Pauls
1600–1	34–5	Marston writes *Antonio and Mellida* and *Antonio's Revenge*, also for the Children of Pauls
?1601	35	Marston writes *What You Will*, also in connection with the War of the Theatres
1602	38	Shakespeare buys more property and land in Stratford
	18	Beaumont's *Hermaphroditus and Salmacis* published anonymously. (None of Beaumont's works printed in his lifetime bore his name.) May also have written the verses signed 'F. B.' and prefixed to his brother John's poem *The Metamorphosis of Tobacco*
	44	Lodge publishes his translation of *The Famous and Memorable Works of Josephus* from Latin and French

Year	Artistic Events	Historical Events
1599	Death of Spenser The burning of various satirical and other works, including Marlowe's *All Ovid's Elegies* and Marston's *The Metamorphosis of Pygmalion's Image*, ordered by the Bishop of London and the Archbishop of Canterbury Globe theatre built on Bankside and the Lord Chamberlain's Men occupy it	Essex sent as Lord Deputy to Ireland, his unauthorised return and disgrace Birth of Oliver Cromwell
1600	Fortune theatre built on Bankside Gilbert, *De Magnete*	Founding of the East India Company
1601		Abortive rising of Essex, and subsequent execution for treason
1602	Founding of the Bodleian Library	

Year	Age	Life
1603	45	Lodge publishes *A Treatise of the Plague*
	39	Shakespeare acts in Jonson's *Sejanus*. Lord Chamberlain's Men taken, with the other dramatic companies, under royal patronage and renamed The King's Men
	37	Marston writes *The Malcontent* (published 1604) initially for the Children of the Revels, then with additions by John Webster for the King's Men; he becomes shareholder in the Children of the Revels until 1608 and writes all his subsequent plays for them
1604	38	Marston collaborates on *Eastward Ho* (performed 1605) with Chapman and Jonson; he gets into trouble with the authorities and may have been briefly imprisoned
		Marlowe's *Dr Faustus* (A text) published posthumously
	40	Shakespeare probably writes *Othello*
1605	39	Marston writes *The Dutch Courtesan*; around this time he marries Mary Wilkes, daughter of a preacher
	41	Shakespeare writes *King Lear*, and soon after this, *Macbeth*
?1605	21	Beaumont collaborates on *Love's Cure* with John Fletcher, the beginning of an important and extensive theatrical partnership. Probably sharing lodgings with Fletcher in Southwark at this time
1606	48	Lodge leaves England to work in Brussels on account of his Catholic sympathies
	22	Beaumont writes *The Woman Hater* (printed 1607), probably with a little assistance from Fletcher
	40	Marston writes *The Fawn*, *Sophonisba*, and *A City Spectacle*, a pageant for King James and his guest, King Christian of Denmark
?1607	23	Beaumont, with Fletcher, writes commendatory verses for Jonson's *Volpone*; he remains a close friend of Jonson for some years. He writes *The Knight of the Burning Pestle* (printed 1613), his only solo play. Although now well-known, it was a failure at the time
1608	42	Marston imprisoned in Newgate; sells shares in the Children of the Revels. Possibly writes unfinished play, *The Insatiate Countess* (completed by William Barksted by 1613)
	44	The King's Men take over the lease of Blackfriars, an indoor theatre; Shakespeare buys a share in it; he probably writes *Pericles*, the first of his romances
?1608	24	Beaumont writes *Cupid's Revenge* (printed 1615) with Fletcher

Year	Artistic Events	Historical Events
1603	Lord Chamberlain's Men taken, along with the other theatrical companies, under royal patronage, and renamed the King's Men Florio's translation of Montaigne's *Essais* Jonson, *Sejanus*	Death of Elizabeth I and accession of James I Outbreak of plague in London
1604		Treaty of London ends Anglo-Spanish War
1605	Bacon, *The Advancement of Learning*	Gunpowder Plot
1606	Jonson, *Volpone* Middleton(?), *The Revenger's Tragedy*	
1607	The King's Men take over the lease of Blackfriars, an indoor theatre, and Shakespeare buys a lease in it Birth of Milton	English settlement in Virginia Land in Ulster given to English and Scottish settlers

Year	Age	Life
1609	43	Marston ordained deacon and subsequently priest at Stanton Harcourt, Oxfordshire
	45	Publication of Shakespeare's *Sonnets* and *A Lover's Complaint*
	25	Beaumont writes various poems, including a verse letter to Ben Jonson from the country, and possibly *The Coxcomb* (printed 1647) as well as *Philaster* (printed 1620) with Fletcher
1610	26	Beaumont writes *The Scornful Lady* (printed 1616) and possibly *The Maid's Tragedy* (printed 1619) with Fletcher in this year
	52	Lodge admitted to the College of Physicians; later returns to England
1611	27	Beaumont writes *A King and No King* (printed 1619) with Fletcher
	47	Shakespeare's *The Winter's Tale* acted, and a performance described by Simon Forman; *The Tempest*, for which Shakespeare draws on the Virginia material, acted at court
1612	28	Beaumont writes his verse elegy for the Countess of Rutland, daughter of Sir Philip Sidney
1613	49	Shakespeare buys property in Blackfriars; collaborates with John Fletcher on *Henry VIII* and *The Two Noble Kinsmen* and retires from the stage; Globe Theatre burns down at a performance of *Henry VIII*, and is rebuilt the next year
	55	Lodge publishes his translation of *The Works both Moral and Natural of Seneca*
	29	Beaumont's *The Masque of Inner Temple and Gray's Inn* performed 20 February. He marries Ursula Isley about this time, and leaves London for Kent
1613–16	29–32	Beaumont writes a second verse epistle to Jonson, 'To Mr B. J.'; possibly continues to contribute in a small way to Fletcher's collaborations with Massinger and others

Year	Artistic Events	Historical Events
1609	Spenser, *The Faerie Queene*, published with the *Cantos of Mutabilitie*	Wreck of the *Sea Adventure*, one of a group of ships on a colonising mission to Virginia, off the coast of the Bermudas
1610	Publication of pamphlets describing the Virginia expedition	
1611	Spenser's *Works* published in folio Authorised version of the *Bible* Chapman completes translation of the *Iliad*	
1612	Webster, *The White Devil*	Death of Prince Henry, King James's heir Bermudas settled by English colonists
1613	Burning down of Globe theatre Webster, *The Duchess of Malfi*	Marriage of James's daughter, Elizabeth, to Frederick, Elector of Palatine Countess of Essex divorced and married to the King's favourite, Robert Carr, Earl of Somerset
1614	Chapman translation of the *Odyssey*, Books 1–12 Raleigh, *The History of the World* Globe theatre rebuilt	Napier invents logarithms
1615	Chapman, translation of the *Odyssey*, Books 13–24	

Year	Age	Life
1616	50	Marston becomes a priest at Christchurch, Hants.
	32	Death of Beaumont, 6 March, buried in Westminster Abbey
	52	Death of Shakespeare at Stratford, buried at Parish church Marlowe's *Dr Faustus* (B text) published posthumously
	58	Lodge leaves England for the Low Countries and practises medicine there until his return in 1619
1621	63	Lodge publishes his translation *A Learned Summary upon the famous Poem of William of Salust Lord of Bartas*
1625	67	Lodge dies, possibly of plague then rife in London

Year	Artistic Events	Historical Events
1616	Jonson's *Works* published in folio James I, *Works*	Trial of Earl and Countess of Somerset for the murder of Sir Thomas Overbury; advancement of James I's new favourite, George Villiers Harvey lectures on his discovery of the circulation of the blood
1618		Beginning of the Thirty Years' War Execution of Raleigh
1620	Bacon, *Novum Organum*	Voyage of the Pilgrim Fathers in the *Mayflower* to America; first African slaves imported to America
1621	Burton, *The Anatomy of Melancholy* Birth of Marvell	First Parliament since 1614 Impeachment of Bacon
1622	Completion of Inigo Jones's Banqueting House at Whitehall Middleton and Rowley, *The Changeling*	James I dissolves Parliament
1623		Prince Charles and Villiers, now Duke of Buckingham, in Madrid negotiating for a Spanish marriage for the Prince; negotiations fail
1624	Donne, *Devotions upon Emergent Occasions*	Virginia becomes a crown colony
1625		Death of James I; succession of his son Charles I, who marries French Catholic Henrietta Maria Plague rife in London
1626	Death of Bacon Sandys's translation of Ovid's *Metamorphoses*	Impeachment of Buckingham, assassinated two years later
1627	Bacon, *The New Atlantis*	
1628	Harvey, *Exercitatio Anatomica de Motu Cordis et Sanguinis in Animalibus* (translated 1653 as *Anatomical Exercises*)	
1629		Charles I dissolves Parliament English settle Massachusetts
1630		Birth of the future Charles II Peace with Spain

Year	Age	Life
1631	65	Marston resigns living at Christchurch, and probably returns to London
1633		Marlowe's *The Jew of Malta* published posthumously
1634	68	Marston's *Collected Plays* published; he dies in London, buried in Temple Church
1640		Beaumont's *Poems* (including some not by Beaumont); reprinted 1653, with additions
1647		Publication of the First Folio of the Beaumont and Fletcher plays, *Comedies and Tragedies*, containing 34 plays and the Masque
1679		Publication of the Second Folio of the Beaumont and Fletcher plays, *Fifty Comedies and Tragedies*, containing 52 plays

Year	Artistic Events	Historical Events
1631	Death of John Donne	
1632	Van Dyke settles in England	
1633	Donne's *Poems* published Death of George Herbert and posthumous publication of *The Temple*	Charles I crowned King of Scotland
1634	Milton, *A Masque (Comus)*	Witch trials in Lancashire

INTRODUCTION

The five poems in this collection were chosen to represent the best examples of a late Elizabethan genre of erotic-mythological poetry which would also be the most appealing to modern readers. They are all the work of young poets who became better known for other sorts of writing, and the poems share a freshness and readiness to experiment which contribute to their charm. The term epyllion, or minor epic, now commonly used for this genre, has long been regarded with suspicion by classicists who disagree as to its validity as a generic label.[1] But it is now an accepted term for a certain kind of narrative poem which combines disparate elements from several genres, is classicising (packed with self-consciously classical references and allusions) and erotic in manner, and devotes itself to an Ovidian-style story of love. It is a much shorter form of narrative than the epic and more limited in its concerns. Though the poets included here would not have used the word 'epyllion', they were certainly conscious of writing in a particular genre, and in what they regarded as the style of Ovid, who was a major influence on the nature of their eroticism.

In the period of about fifteen years at the end of the sixteenth century when these poems were being written, the meanings that educated English readers associated with the name of Ovid were changing. Chaucer had known him as 'Venus' clerk Ovide', but the vigorous medieval tradition of subjecting Ovid's poems to moralising commentary died hard. The first English printed translation of Ovid, the anonymous *Fable of Ovid Treting of Narcissus* (1560) follows up 192 lines of jingling poulter's metre with a series of long stanzas that liken Narcissus in his sin of pride to conventional examples of proud folk who come to a bad end, such as Samson and Cleopatra. The poem also points out that Ovid could be an improving poet if read correctly.

Golding's influential translation of the complete *Metamorphoses* (1567), dedicated to the Puritan Earl of Leicester, contained a preface with interpretations of the stories that give them a specifically Christian slant. The anxiety about the potentially corrupting effects of Ovid's licentiousness, which the stress on specialised interpretation sought to conceal, also surfaced in the later part of the sixteenth century. Preachers denounced the reading of erotic poets, including 'a great part of Ovid',[2] and Marlowe's translation of Ovid's *Amores* (though not *Hero and Leander*) was ordered to be burnt by the ecclesiastical authorities in 1599. In 1582 the Privy Council, hoping to raise moral standards, prescribed patriotic literature for boys in grammar schools, instead of 'Ovid de arte amandi, de tristibus or suche lyke'. But in view of the flood of Ovidian verse produced in the next two decades, and the enthusiasm with which it was received, this was to little avail. When Francis Meres recorded exuberantly in 1598 that 'the sweete witty soule of Ovid lives in mellifluous and honey-tongued Shakespeare, witness his *Venus and Adonis*', he seemed to be speaking for his times, or at least for the educated and the avant-garde.

Ovidian mythologising was a fashion, and, like all fashions, when in decline it was sneered at and denigrated. Thomas Carew's 'Elegy upon the death of . . . Dr John Donne' praised Donne for making Ovidian poetry a thing of the past; Donne and his followers scorned the 'silenc'd tales o' th' Metamorphoses'. Nonetheless the two best-known Ovidian poems, *Venus and Adonis* and *Hero and Leander*, continued to be reprinted for several years to come. No doubt the equivocal reputation they acquired was part of their attraction for some. The student, Gullio, in the university play *The Return from Parnassus* puts *Venus and Adonis* under his pillow at night, while Middleton's disapproving citizen Harebrain in *A Mad World, My Masters* (1613) coupled the two poems as 'two luscious marrow-bones for a young married wife'. This racy aura lingered on for some time. In a poem of 1635 called *Amanda, or The Reformed Whore* by Thomas Cranley, Amanda's library, before her reformation, consists of 'amorous pamphlets' and

> Songs of love and Sonets exquisit:
> Among these Venus and Adonis lies,
> With Salmacis and her Hermaphrodit,
> Pigmalion's there with his transform'd delight.

Ovid's poetry extended over a range of genres, and the Elizabethans translated from the *Amores* and the *Heroides* as well as the *Metamorphoses*, but it is Ovid's major work, his epic composed in the wake of Virgil's *Aeneid*, which is seminal for an understanding of these poems by Lodge, Shakespeare, Marlowe, Beaumont and Marston. The *Metamorphoses* inspired the Elizabethan poets in many ways. It provided a model for a non-linear narrative structure, and it represented a special kind of interaction between human life and the natural and supernatural worlds. It also spoke of human sexuality in terms which seemed relevant and challenging at a time when various forces, such as Puritanism, humanist culture, and the power over her people's imaginations exercised by the Virgin Queen, combined to unsettle and even change accepted attitudes to love, marriage, and gender relationships. Ovid's bold and often shocking depictions in the *Metamorphoses* of the effects of sexual desire appealed particularly to young writers interested in questioning the conventions of Petrarchanism.*

Within a chronological framework that extends from the creation of the world to the death and deification of Augustus Caesar, Ovid interweaves an enormous collection of separate legends, proceeding by means of recollections and parallels, episodes within episodes, digressions and juxtapositions. Not only does he use a variety of narrators, who lend their own colouring to the stories they relate, but he explains in words tales that were originally rendered in some other medium – woven into a tapestry, for example, or embossed on a bowl. The Elizabethan poets imitate these narrative techniques in their own manner. In *Scylla's Metamorphosis* the narrator begins by telling his own story but breaks off to allow Glaucus to tell his, and the poem does not return to the original tale until the final stanza. In the epyllia of Shakespeare, Marlowe, and Beaumont, digressions disrupt the straightforward momentum of the main story and become engrossing narratives in their own right. In all of them the story as such is often suspended to create opportunities for rhetorical display: when Venus and Adonis debate the nature of love and lust, for example, or Leander shows off his sophistical skills in arguing against the preservation of virginity.

Ovid was self-conscious about his material in the sense that he treated the Greek legends quite openly as fictions devised to explain or account for certain aspects of reality, and he regarded the gods and goddesses who people them with comic detachment. But there is nothing comforting or domesticated about his conception of the natural world, anthropomorphic though it is. The Elizabethan poets adopt completely Ovid's view of the gods as beings who are alarming in their combination of supernatural power and violent passion – forces which animate the natural world. Yet these gods are not omnipotent in matters of love, and they cannot always oblige mortals to accede to their wishes. The wayward nature of erotic desire is a major theme in Ovid, and it constitutes the mainspring of these five poems. In all of them Venus, and not Cupid, is invoked as presiding deity: as 'Paphian Queen of love/Mistress of sweet conspiring harmony' by Lodge, as lover of Adonis and Mars by Marlowe, as 'Sacred Queen of sportive dallying' by Marston, and as muse of his verses by Beaumont. She is of course Shakespeare's protagonist. The sea-born goddess, a powerfully sexual presence, is a more appropriate symbol of love than her playful son.

The eroticism of these poems is one reason for the queasiness about them in much criticism of the earlier part of this century. It is a good reason for taking a fresh look at them now, during a period of changing awareness of how sexuality is represented in literature, particularly that of Shakespeare and Marlowe's time. Ovid's *Ars Amatoria* and *Amores* gave him a reputation as an 'amorous schoolmaster', as Stephen Gosson called him disapprovingly, a characterisation that is reinforced in the *Metamorphoses*, with its depictions of the gods 'in sundry shapes, committing heady riots, incest, rapes' (*Hero and Leander*, 1, 143–4). These Elizabethan poems render Ovidian eroticism in terms of their own preoccupations. They concern themselves with the transformational power of desire in several ways, and with the disruption it brings to conventional power-structures in relationships. Gods find themselves impotent in the face of mortal obduracy and women, overcome with desire, abandon all modesty in order to pursue young men who are colder than any Petrarchan lady of the sonnets. 'Alas sweet nymphs, my godhead's all in vain', laments Lodge's Glaucus, who can charm the winds and waters but not the heart of Scylla: 'She's Love, she loves, and yet she is not lov'd', comments the narrator of *Venus and Adonis* on the frustrated goddess. Beaumont's Salmacis, 'almost mad' with desire for coy Hermaphroditus as she watches him taking off his clothes beside a pool, jumps in and does her best to rape him.

A basic source of eroticism in the poems is the reversal of accepted gender-roles which comes about when the reluctance of the man obliges the woman who desires him to act as wooer. This challenge to the conventions of heterosexual courtship is emphasised by the particular nature of the man's sexuality. His Ovidian model is Ganymede or Narcissus: he is inexperienced and very young (in Hermaphroditus' case, specifically fifteen); he is irresistably beautiful with long hair and a smooth pale body, and he arouses desire in men and women alike. His homoerotic appeal is defined most explicitly in Marlowe's Leander:

> Some swore he was a maid in man's attire
> For in his looks were all that men desire.
>
> (ll. 83–4)

But such qualities are also evident in Shakespeare's 'rose-cheek'd Adonis' and Beaumont's Hermaphroditus:

> Like iv'ry then his snowy body was,
> Or a white lily in a crystal glass
>
> (ll. 863–4)

as well as in a host of ambiguous youths like Drayton's Endimion, who looks like a nymph in boy's clothes, Weever's Faunus, and Phineas Fletcher's Anchises. In Marlowe's poem and those of his imitators, the youth's sexual innocence is equalled by the girl's. For the poem's narrator and, by implication, for the sophisticated reader, there is both comedy and titillation in their gauche and fumbling encounters:

> . . . Leander, rude in love, and raw,
> Long dallying with Hero, nothing saw
> That might delight him more, yet he suspected
> Some amorous rites or other were neglected.
>
> (ll. 61–4)

In Shakespeare's poem the youth who is not only inexperienced but also reluctant is matched with an amorous and powerful woman who has a range of wooing techniques to command, but nonetheless can win nothing more from him than a good night kiss. In the literature of this period the figure of the actively desiring woman elicits a variety of responses, some of which are represented in the epyllia. For Lodge's Scylla, for instance, frustrated desire is imposed on her as a punishment for previous sexual resistance and as a prelude to petrific metamorphosis. Salmacis's wooing of Hermaphroditus, by contrast, is handled in a direct and erotic manner as the nymph fondles each part of the boy's 'white and youthfull' body in turn. Somewhere between the two comes Shakespeare's Venus who at one moment invites Adonis to explore her body in elegant topographical metaphor –

> I'll be a park, and thou shalt be my deer:
> Feed where thou wilt, on mountain or in dale—

and at another ravenous and sweating, devours him with kisses as hungrily as a starved bird of prey.

Implicitly, and sometimes explicitly, these poets acknowledge a range of sexual proclivities in their readers, though always making it clear that the readership is defined as sophisticated, educated, and, of course, male. Knowing narrators, like those of Beaumont, Marlowe, and his imitators, draw the reader into masculine collusion with misogynistic asides: 'All women are ambitious naturally', (*Hero and Leander*, l. 428); 'Women may be likened to the year/Whose first fruits still do make the daintiest cheer' (*Salmacis and Hermaphroditus*, ll. 143–4); 'In women's mouths, No is no negative' (*The Metamorphosis of Pygmalion's Image*, l. 310). But the poems appeal to, and stimulate, several kinds of sexual fantasy: Beaumont in his dream of androgyny – and perhaps Shakespeare in articulating the frustrations of his goddess of love – explore what it might mean to break down the physical boundaries of gender; Marlowe, through his description of Neptune's impassioned underwater wooing of Leander, expresses a sense of the overwhelming effect of desire; Marston's story of Pygmalion bringing his ivory statue to life through the strength of his desire realises the male myth of irresistible sexual potency. The poems also appeal to other areas of the imagination in their sensuously rich and eclectic evocation of the world of classical myth and legend. Above all, in the poetic and rhetorical inventiveness with which they expand brief episodes from Ovid, they illustrate that myth-making impulse which was so strong for all Renaissance poets and the desire to interpret the past in terms of the present.

Lodge, *Scylla's Metamorphosis*

For the general reader, *Scylla's Metamorphosis* is unlikely to be much more than a footnote to literary history. Neither its narrative momentum nor, in modern terms, its erotic content is high. There are some dainty descriptions of nymphs in the standard style of Elizabethan sensuousness which might remind us now of the lusciously classical paintings of J. W. Waterhouse or Lord Leighton. Scylla's charms are formally itemised in terms of apple-like breasts, marble flanks, and a 'milk-white bank' sheltering a hidden fountain, but in general the poem's appeal is more to the lover of rhetorical patterning than to the lover of the human body. On the other hand, anyone interested in the literary and cultural context of the better known epyllia, particularly of *Venus and Adonis*, will find this early work of Lodge – probably written when the doctor-to-be was still in his twenties – revelatory. There can be no doubt that Shakespeare had read the poem, and his imagination was stirred by the stanzas on Venus and the dying Adonis (21–23) which sound so many of the keynotes of his own work – the colour contrasts of pallor and blood, the pathos of the delicate flower-like youth, the hopeless grief of the bereaved goddess. He also adopted Lodge's six-line stanza form. But by looking at what he did not take from Lodge, we can see how Lodge's handling of mythological material reveals itself as in many ways tentative and insecure.

For instance, Lodge's framework for his tale of Ovidian transformation is the medieval love-complaint, narrated by a love-sick speaker trying to find consolation for his suffering. Not only is the narrator weeping for unrequited love as he wanders by the river Isis, but the sea-god Glaucus, also rather incongruously discovered in this setting, is even more distraught because of his rejection by the proud nymph Scylla. The poem brims over with tears and lamentations: the rocks weep and the birds are pensive, the nymphs grieve until Themis, Glaucus' mother, 'with sorrowing sobs' begs Venus to come to her son's rescue. The result is that Glaucus is cured, but now it is Scylla's turn to sigh and plead and rend her hair when Cupid shoots her with his arrow and she falls in love with Glaucus. She withdraws to a rocky den to give voice to her lamentations and is transformed by furies from the underworld to a sea-monster eternally imprisoned in a gloomy pool encircled by howling winds.

Claims have been made for elements of parody and comic exaggeration in the poem, which is one way of making it seem more accessible to an ironic late-twentieth century sensibility, but this idea fails to reckon with the Elizabethan taste for rhetorical display for its own sake. Although by no means Lodge's first published work, *Scylla's Metamorphosis* has a distinct air of self-conscious experimentation about it. The poet is showing what he can do with rhetorical schemes like ana-phora*. (stanzas 1, 104, 105), paradox* (stanza 59), and chiasmus* (stanza 31); formulaic devices like the blazon of female beauty (stanzas 48–53); erotic punning (stanzas 15–16), and a variety of metrical techniques. He can deploy feminine rhymes* as well as Marlowe (stanza 54), and he can modulate from his basically iambic line into lyrical dactyls* where appro-priate (stanza 59). The world of myth is evoked allusively, with knowing periphrases that set up a collusion between a poet sophisticated enough to wear his learning lightly and a well-educated reader sufficiently familiar with 'the sweet Arcadian boy' (Adonis), and the 'ivory brow' of 'the Theban' (Apollo) not to need the characters identified by name. The descriptive manner recalls the richness of Renaissance tapestries, 'costly clothes of Arras and of Toure' as Spenser calls those in his House of Malecasta in *The Faerie Queene* which depict the story of Venus and Adonis: the arrival of Themis and her sea-nymphs gliding 'upon the silver bosom of the stream'; the visitation of Venus in her embroidered robes; winged Cupid seated on her lap; and finally the transformation of sorrowing Scylla herself:

> her locks
> Are changed with wonder into hideous sands,
> And hard as flint become her snow-white hands
> (ll. 736–8)

Lodge in fact considerably modifies the story of Scylla as he found it in Ovid, omitting much of the grotesquerie of the metamorphosis: Ovid, partly following Homer, has Scylla changed by the power of Circe first into a monster, woman to the waist and a mass of barking dogs beneath, and subsequently into a rocky reef (*Metamorphoses* XIV). Lodge follows up his brief account of Scylla's demise with a moralising couplet from his narrator, who applies the myth to his own situation as a frustrated lover:

> Ah, nymphs, thought I, if every coy one felt
> The like mishaps, their flinty hearts would melt.
>
> (ll. 749–50)

Lodge concludes the poem with an envoy addressed to women urging them to avoid a Scylla-like punishment for 'women's proud backsliding' by being more sexually generous; but his imaginative interest does not seem to be fully absorbed in the poetic exploration of the tension between the incompatible desires of divinities and human beings. The tradition of Ovid moralised is acknowledged by Lodge, but the poem is more concerned with what the narrator calls 'feeling words' and 'working lines' (stanza 73), and with the relation between feeling and aesthetic expression. The poem's elaborate structure whereby the poet-narrator, about to recount his own love-sorrows, is absorbed instead into the story of Glaucus and Scylla and taught a lesson in love, doubly distances the myth from the reader and puts into the foreground the whole issue of how poetry can handle feeling. Like Sidney in *Astrophel and Stella*, which Lodge might conceivably have known in manuscript, Lodge believes that the fictionalising of emotion will be more effective in moving the reader than a plain and direct account: 'I am not I, pity the tale of me', as Astrophel says in Sonnet 45 urging Stella to respond to the story of his love, if she cannot love him directly. While a modern reader may accept the viewpoint, he or she will not necessarily react emotionally to the rhetorical means Lodge employs in his fiction. Nonetheless the poem provides an illuminating preface to the more accessible imaginative world of Shakespeare.

Shakespeare, *Venus and Adonis*

Although Shakespeare was obviously inspired by Lodge's 'Fair Venus in her ivory coach', this stately and omnipotent deity is quite unlike his own protagonist. Not for nothing did this poem quickly acquire the reputation of a lover's *vade mecum*. It was Shakespeare's first published work, printed in 1593 with a dedication to the Earl of Southampton in which he called it 'the first heir of my invention'. The title-page couplet from Ovid's *Amores* suggests that he was making a bid for the fame and reputation of a serious writer, perhaps to counter Greene's insulting description of him the previous year as an 'upstart crow' on the London stage:

> Vilia miretur vulgus; mihi flavus Apollo
> Pocula Castalia plena ministret acqua.

In Marlowe's translation this reads: 'Let base-conceited wits admire vile things,/Fair Phoebus lead me to the Muses'springs.'

The poem was immediately popular and successful, imitated only a few months after its appearance by Thomas Edwards in his poem *Cephalus and Procris*. In Shakespeare's lifetime it was the most often alluded to and quoted of all his works, though critics in our own century have found much to puzzle over and less to admire. The story of Venus's love for Adonis and his death in a boar-hunt comes from *Metamorphoses* (X, 519–59, 705–39), which Shakespeare knew in Latin although he also draws on Golding's translation. Adonis's reluctance is not in this particular tale of Ovid's, but it may come instead from the stories of Salmacis and Hermaphroditus (*Metamorphoses* IV, 347–481) or of Echo and Narcissus (*Metamorphoses* III, 427–542, 635–42), which both provide models for the self-loving young man attempting to evade an amorous woman's pursuit. But the two figures are not stereotypes, and Shakespeare's depiction of their relationship, fired by his imaginative understanding of their sexuality, is equally sensitive to their contrasting predicaments.

A number of critics have written disparagingly of the poem for its handling of Venus, without showing any consciousness of biases created by the patriarchal tradition from which their own assumptions about female sexuality have come. Coleridge's unease with the poem's offbeat eroticism bears a lot of the responsibility here. C. S. Lewis is blunter than most, but not atypical in his standpoint when he objects to Venus because she reminds him of 'horrible interviews with voluminous female relatives in one's early childhood'. Similarly, John Buxton finds her passion for the much younger Adonis 'abnormal, unnatural, and disgusting', but does not question why his own response to the poem is so different from that of its first readers.[3] Shakespeare's goddess is confusingly multi-faceted, being at one point large enough to tuck Adonis under her arm (ll. 31–2) and at another so delicate that she can 'dance on the sands, and yet no footing seen' (l. 148). She smothers him with kisses like a ravenous eagle devouring its prey, sweating, panting; yet all the time she is incarnating the spirit of love so light that it can fly through the sky in a chariot drawn by doves. Voluptuous and alluring, her flesh is 'soft and plump' (l. 142), her body, in one of the poem's most quoted passages (ll. 229–240) is a fertile terrain for a lover to explore. She is active and passive, mother and mistress, lover and beloved, all in one. The expression of her passion for the unresponsive youth is sometimes comic, sometimes pitiable in its misdirected strength. Shakespeare plays on the paradoxical concept of the female wooer – the woman taking the role that society conventionally assigns to the man – to explore the condition of sexual frustration: 'Backward she push'd him, as she would be thrust' (l. 41). Yet, for all her erotic enticements, Venus cannot arouse Adonis's desire: she pushes her lover to the ground, pulls him on top of her, forces him into the position of copulation, but being a woman she cannot rape him. Shakespeare makes it clear that the imbalance between desire and the physical means to realise it is the source of Venus's pain:

> Now is she in the very lists of love,
> Her champion mounted for the hot encounter,
> All is imaginary she doth prove:
> He will not manage her, although he mount her;
>   That worse than Tantalus' is her annoy,
>   To clip Elysium and to lack her joy.
>
>   (ll. 595–600)

The poem abounds in the figures of antithesis and paradox, used not simply as devices of rhetorical display but as means to explore the condition of sexual frustration. The lovers are opposite in their desires, if similar in their displays of feeling: 'She red and hot as coals of glowing fire,/He red for shame, but frosty in desire' (l. 36). Joined by a kiss, they are dissatisfied for exactly opposite reasons: 'He with her plenty press'd, she faint with dearth' (l. 545).

Adonis's situation is almost as unhappy as Venus's, and his image in the poem is self-contradictory: he appears at times like the 'wanton female boy' of Gaveston's fantasy in Marlowe's *Edward II*, 'rose-cheek'd', 'sweet above compare ... more

lovely than a man' (l. 9); he is dimpled and bonneted like
Donatello's dainty figure of David; but he is also clumsy, gauche,
sullen – '[he] blush'd and pouted in a dull disdain' (l. 33) –
louring and graceless. For Venus he represents 'fruitless chast-
ity', like the young man in the first sonnets of Shakespeare's
sequence, who, by refusing to procreate denies the world the use
(in the complex sense of profit obtained through creative econ-
omics) of his beauty. In an image of transience that acquires the
status of leitmotif in the poem, he is likened to 'the field's chief
flower' which will rot away and leave no trace, like Narcissus
who dies of self-love. Adonis's counter-argument to Venus's
persuasions to love, that he is unripe and unready – like an
incomplete garment or plant in bud – are given less rhetorical
weight in the poem, and his preference for boar-hunting over
love, leads directly to his death.

The account of hunting in Shakespeare's poem partakes both
of the ancient world of myth – with its ominous image of the
glowing-eyed, bloody-fanged boar, an alternative lover to Venus,
eagerly sheathing its tusks in the youth's 'soft groin' – and of the
contemporary world of the Warwickshire countryside. Venus's
stanzas about 'poor Wat', the purblind hare, hunted by 'hot
scent-sniffing hounds' over hills and valleys, have moved many
readers in their fresh evocation of an English rural life that owes
nothing to classical pastoral. This two-fold resonance is charac-
teristic of the poem as a whole. On the other hand it is a
sophisticated piece of myth-making, which retells a familiar story
of the loves of 'powerful gods', as Marlowe puts it, with a new
twist. It culminates in a neatly handled aetiology (a fictional
account of the causes or origins of something accepted as a fact
of life) of the sorrows of love, which Venus ascribes to Adonis's
premature death. On the other hand, the poem is an English
pastoral filled with images of country creatures and pastimes,
from the hunted hare and the snail, the netted bird and the
divedapper (or dabchick) peeping out of the water, to Adonis's
restive horse breaking free to gallop away through the woods
with a jennet while crows wheel overhead. Shakespeare acknowl-
edges the convention of representing the natural world through
mythology, as, for example, in the poem's opening lines –

> Even as the sun with purple-colour'd face
> Takes his last leave of the weeping morn—

which depict sunrise in terms of Phoebus the sungod leaving the bed of Aurora, goddess of dawn, but he takes the idea of localising his action in a native setting much further than Lodge. This together with the vividly realised physicality of the lovers – sweating, blushing, rolling on the ground – and so forth, makes it difficult to accept moralistic readings of the kind that have been proposed for the poem: that it is an allegory about the fatal effects of lust, for example, or that Venus is punished for transgressing the norms of feminine behaviour.[4] The detachment of the narrative voice is thrown into relief by the large proportion of speech in the poem, much of it in emotionally coloured modes such as persuasion or debate. The conclusion, in which Adonis's body disappears and from his shed blood springs a purple flower which Venus promptly gathers and takes away with her as she flies off to Paphos, evades metamorphosis and is markedly unjudgmental. The goddess leaves a world where love can never exist without pain and suffering and goes into retreat.

Marlowe, *Hero and Leander*

The exact nature of the relationship between Shakespeare's epyllion and Marlowe's may remain forever unknown, since there is as yet no evidence to prove which was written first. *Hero and Leander* was entered in the Stationers' Register in September 1593, four months after the poet's death, but not published until 1598; though evidently it was already known to contemporaries by then. The poem appears to be unfinished, and the two cantos, or, as the publisher calls them, sestiads, which Marlowe wrote are followed by the words '*desunt nonulla*' (something is lacking). A conclusion in three further sestiads was supplied by George Chapman extremely different in style and manner. 'Love's edge is taken off', wrote Chapman, accurately summarising the change. The tragic story of Hero and Leander derives not from Ovid, although he does use it in *Heroides* XVIII and XIX, but from the fifth-century Alexandrian Greek poet Musaeus, widely believed in Marlowe's time to have been one of the legendary founders of Greek poetry, even the son and pupil of Orpheus himself. Musaeus's epyllion had been translated into Latin, French, Italian and Spanish, and the story itself was probably better known than that of Venus and Adonis. Marlowe's choice of subject suggests ambition: a desire to present his own version of a story at which many masters had already tried their hands, and one associated with the very origins of poetry itself.

Like *Venus and Adonis, Hero and Leander* was a 'master-piece' in the old sense of an example in miniature of a crafts-man's skills, designed to prove he had attained to the status of 'master'. But in many ways the poem is very different, in tone, mood, narrative method and, most obviously, in poetic form. Marlowe decided against the six-line stanzas used by Lodge, Shakespeare, and later Marston, and chose instead pentameter couplets, which have the effect of moving the action along much faster and of providing a sense of brevity and condensation. They also present many opportunities for comic rhyme:

> At last, like to a bold sharp sophister,
> With cheerful hope, thus he accosted her
> > (ll. 197–8)
>
> Or thirsting after immortalitie
> All women are ambitious naturally –
> > (ll. 427–8)
>
> She with a kind of granting put him by it
> And ever as he thought himself most nigh it
> Like to the tree of Tantalus she fled,
> And seeming lavish, sav'd her maidenhead.
> > (ll. 73–6)

Not only did Marlowe, like Byron in *Don Juan*, make comedy from the effects of a wrenched accent in a feminine rhyme, but, as in the last example, he followed feminine rhymes by mascu-line rhymes* to produce an epigrammatic wit. In general *Hero and Leander* is more witty than *Venus and Adonis*, and the wit, often contained in the observations of a wryly knowing narrator, is an integral part of the imaginative world of the poem. The four lines in which Marlowe alludes (without naming him) to the story of Narcissus, perfectly encapsulates this aspect of Marlowe's style. Thus his 'slack muse' sings of Leander's beauty:

> Those orient cheekes and lips, exceeding his
> That leapt into the water for a kiss
> Of his own shadow, and despising many
> Died ere he could enjoy the love of any.
> > (ll. 73–6)

The allusion is irreverent in its periphrasis for Narcissus and in its attitude to classical mythology ('a flippancy in a conducted tour of the glories that were Greece', as one critic puts it). The feminine rhyme, turning 'many' and 'any' into opposites, mocks Narcissus' predicament and lightens the otherwise sombre note of tragic anticipation in its dismissive attitude towards dying for love or leaping into the water for a kiss (as, in a sense, Leander will do).

But comic detachment is only one strand in the poem's strange and complex tonal harmony. Although Marlowe never brought his love-story to the tragic conclusion his readers would have been prepared for, his handling of the loves of gods and men does not avoid absurdity or love's propensity for frustration and humiliation. Hero and Leander are inept as lovers, often comically so. Leander thinks himself as sophisticated in erotic strategy as he is in rhetoric, but in the event proves himself an inexperienced virgin:

> this jewel he enjoy'd
> And as a brother with his sister toy'd
> Supposing nothing else was to be done
> (ll. 51–3)

Hero alternates conventionally feminine flirtatiousness – dropping her fan, inviting Leander to visit her by an apparent slip of the tongue – with genuine shyness – shrieking aloud when she finds him at her door without his clothes. But with self-concealing mastery Marlowe rapidly modulates into another mode when at the end of the poem he describes the sexual consummation. Hero in Leander's arms trembles like a nervous bird held in the hands, and the urgency of Leander's desire overcomes any wish to spare her feelings:

> Love is not full of pity, as men say,
> But deaf and cruel where he means to prey.
> (ll. 287–8)

The astonishing beauty of Marlowe's lines describing Hero's blushing when she wakes in the morning and tries to escape Leander's gaze does not conceal in their hyperbole the fact that Hero is embarrassed and ashamed, unable to deal with a new and momentous experience. Perhaps because Hero is so clearly a victim, critics have tended to be kinder to her than to Shakespeare's Venus. She is, as one of them has said, 'a woman exposed'.[5] The poem captures the ecstasy of passion as well as

the pain and frustration; and in this gods are treated no
differently from mortals. The representations of Olympian
amours in the statuary and carvings of Venus's temple are of
erotic anarchy: Jove is shown 'bellowing' and 'tumbling' for
love, and rape, incest, and homoeroticism are also depicted.
Mercury, in the poem's first digression, can get nowhere with
the country maid whom he fails to rape, and Neptune, in a
virtuoso passage in Sestiad II, can neither win Leander's interest
nor bring himself to be revenged upon the reluctant youth. The
gods share a human readiness to succumb to erotic delusion.
Against all evidence, Neptune persuades himself that Leander
really is fond of him:

> Love is too full of faith, too credulous,
> With folly and false hope deluding us.
> (ll. 221–2)

The homoerotic element which Shakespeare half reveals, half
conceals in Adonis – a 'youth more lovely than a man', wooed
by a woman who employs male sexual tactics – is more overt in
Leander, whose appeal – to Neptune, to 'wild Hippolytus', to
'the barbarous Thracian soldier' and the innocent Hero – is
more clearly bisexual. Indeed Leander, like Beaumont's Herma-
phroditus, more nearly approximates to the concept of an erotic
ideal without gender identity, an innocent and beautiful ado-
lescent awaiting sexual initiation. Like the poem itself, Leander
seems poised between two conceptions of nature, neither
achieved: heterosexuality, and an undifferentiated sexual energy
which propels gods and mortals alike to seek fulfilment.

The glamorous pictorial qualities of the poem hardly need
pointing out since they compose its rich surface; where Shake-
speare sets his characters in the English countryside, Marlowe's
inhabit a world of artifice created from images of jewels, fabrics,
classical landscapes and legendary beings. Hero and Leander are
like dainty figures from a tapestry or a painting by Fra Angelico
– Elizabethanised versions of classic figures with their bonnets,
fans, kirtles, and buskins. Yet the remoteness and artifice of this
poetic world is tempered, not only by the unease and even the
violence of the passions that break out of it, but also by an
insistent note of satire in the poem. The narrator's comments
and parenthetical interventions (especially his misogynistic
asides) exhibit this satiric edge, but it emerges most explicitly in

the long digression that concludes the first sestiad. The section, a mock-aetiology, reveals the reasons not only for the Fates' hatred of Cupid, but also for scholars always being poor and learning unvalued. The self-reflexive quality here ironically recalls Lodge's narrator vowing in the final stanza of *Scylla's Metamorphosis*, 'to write no more of that whence shame doth grow', but instead to devote himself to the pursuit of fame. Marlowe's poem seems to comment, perhaps rather bitterly, on such literary pretension.

Beaumont, *Salmacis and Hermaphroditus*

Salmacis and Hermaphroditus was published anonymously in 1602, some time after the major fashion for erotic epyllia was over and perhaps this is why Beaumont, then an unknown writer, did not use it to stake his claim to poetic status, as Lodge and Shakespeare had done. The myth of the water-nymph Salmacis who pursues the beautiful but reluctant Hermaphroditus and unites with him only in a pool where their two bodies are transformed into a single bisexual being is a key one for this genre. And the androgynously appealing and sexually innocent male desired by the sexually voracious female is a model for gender relations in many epyllia. In fact one of the earliest sixteenth-century versions of Ovid is Thomas Peend's *The Pleasant Fable of Hermaphroditus and Salmacis ... with a morall in English Verse* (1565), which retells the story as a misogynistic example of the pernicious effects of women's lust. Peend summarises the story as follows:

> Such be the fond and frantike fits
>   which in the blinded brayne
> Of wanton women often times,
>   with swinging swey doth reigne.

Although Beaumont's style is far removed from this, he does not attempt to evade the misogynist emphasis of Ovid's original tale (*Metamorphoses* IV, 285–388) which is narrated as an explanation for the emasculating powers of the pool in which Salmacis and Hermaphroditus have been united. And his own narrator often shares the wryly misogynist tone of Marlowe, whose influence on this poem is pervasive. On the other hand, Beaumont, unlike Peend, is able to take a playful perspective on the Ovidian theme of the unstable boundaries between the genders; he writes in the prefatory lines addressed by 'the author to the reader':

> I hope my poem is so lively writ
>   That thou wilt turne half-maid with reading it.

The reader, needless to say, is imagined as male. The homoerotic appeal of the poem owes much to Marlowe, and Beaumont is equally ready to acknowledge that both sexes will be tantalised by his description of his male protagonist's beauty. At the climax of the poem the reader watches, along with Salmacis who is hidden in the grass, while the fifteen year-old Hermaphroditus strips the clothes from his ivory body and stands naked on the river bank before jumping into the water. The youth is as much the object of the reader's gaze as of the nymph's irresistible desire. The description of Salmacis's detailed contact with Hermaphroditus' body alludes to the rhetorical technique of itemising a woman's body, but the poem transforms the formal catalogue of beauties into a powerfully physical account of amorous foreplay. As the girl touches the boy's skin, hands, chin and lips, action and interaction imitate the rhythms of sex:

> Then did she lift her hand unto his breast,
> A part as white and youthful as the rest,
> Where, as his flowery breath still comes and goes,
> She felt his gentle heart pant through his clothes.
>   (ll. 796–9)

Like Marlowe's Leander striving to escape from Neptune, Hermaphroditus, 'inclaspt in wanton Salmacis' hands', is a youth struggling against the power of a stronger adult lover; but this time the ambiguous sexual desire which the episode arouses is satisfied in a graphic way when the two bodies are merged into one.

In some kinds of writing of the period androgyny is a philosophical ideal, originating in Plato's story in the *Symposium* where mankind's division into two sexes was a punishment. Spenser, for example, in *The Faerie Queene*, uses the hermaphrodite to symbolise the complete union of married lovers in body and soul. The Salmacis and Hermaphroditus story, however, was not usually handled in this way, and certainly this is not the perspective Beaumont takes in his poem where the protagonists are described as 'a luckless pair ... crossed by the sad stars of nativity'. Nor is the poem a subversion of received moralised readings of the story that one might have expected. The ending is somewhat ambiguous, and it has been thought[6] that Beaumont changed his source so as to represent Hermaphroditus as a dying man, thus bringing his story closer to the Narcissus model, and presenting the conjunction of male and female as sterile and deathly. But this rather conflicts with Beaumont's wish to turn his reader 'half-mad' with identificatory pleasure, and there is certainly a conscious irony about the fact that Salmacis and Hermaphroditus already possess characteristics of the opposite sex before they are merged. He is effeminately beautiful, doted on by Apollo and perceiving himself as a 'beauteous Nymph' when reflected in Salmacis' eyes (l. 690), while she imagines herself wooing him 'with manly boldness' (l. 714), and addresses him with the eloquent persuasions to love usually coming from male speakers (like Leander). Their similarities are also pointed up by physical description, of their bodies, and especially their hair (155–8, 105–8, 115–6), and by their shared affinity with water. It is Hermaphroditus' search

> for clear watery springs to bathe him in
> (For he did love to wash his ivory skin)
> (ll. 87–8)

which brings him to the brook where Salmacis lives, preferring to 'wash her snowy limbs' (l. 376) and narcissistically admire her reflection rather than hunt with Diana and her fellow-nymphs. Consequently their fate may be seen as reward as much as punishment. The scene sardonically literalises the cliché of two lovers united in passion, just as Lodge's account of Scylla's petrification does the Petrarchan image of the cold, heartless mistress.

Beaumont's poem shares much more with Marlowe than erotic detail; the vision of chaotic and, for the most part, frustrated, sexual feelings amongst gods who are hightly susceptible to them, and the sense of an anarchic world motivated by appetite are Marlovian, as is the prominent tone of satire. These aspects are displayed in two episodes so lengthy that it is hard to regard them as digressions since together they comprise nearly half the poem and suggest the way that, by Beaumont's time, the balance of interest in the epyllion between the erotic and the satiric, which had always been present, was starting to shift in favour of the latter. In the first episode, Jove's efforts to persuade Salmacis to sleep with him involve a visit to Astraea's court in the skies, an intervention in the marital strife of Venus and Vulcan, and even a power struggle with Vulcan who threatens to deprive Jove of his supply of thunderbolts unless the god gives up his pursuit of the nymph. Jove, king of the gods, is as piqued as any mortal lover at the prospect of abandoning the object of his desire:

> At once he thought, rather than lose her blisses,
> Her heavenly sweets, her most delicious kisses,
> Her soft embraces, and the amorous nights,
> That he should often spend in her delights,
> He would be quite thrown down by mortal hands
> From the blessed place where his bright palace stands
>
> (ll 341–5)

But after weighing up the indignity involved in losing the means to enforce his power over mortals, he reluctantly decides to give up Salmacis but compensates by doubling her beauty. The episode stresses the sexual authority of women in that all the men's activity is motivated by the need to please them in order to obtain sexual favours, and it is Venus's jealousy of Salmacis which ultimately thwarts Jove. In addition, Jove's visit to the palace of Astraea – the virgin goddess of justice regularly used in the late sixteenth century to symbolise Queen Elizabeth – emphasises Astraea's supreme power but also satirises both the image of the Queen (then, of course, in her declining days) and the Elizabethan legal processes, which are depicted as heavily dependent on bribery and corruption. The second episode (this time stemming from Bacchus' efforts to seduce Salmacis) concerns rivalry and revenge among the gods. Once again Salmacis emerges the winner, since Apollo provides her with a beautiful lover (Hermaphroditus) in return for her help in settling his old feud with Mercury.

Beaumont's wit and inventiveness in these sections of the poem exemplify the easy familiarity of these poets with the world of classical myth, and their ability to handle it on their own terms. But although *Salmacis and Hermaphroditus* has its basis in Ovid, its exploration of relationships between the sexes, playfully subversive of late-Elizabethan Petrarchanism remains provocative.

Marston, *The Metamorphosis of Pygmalion's Image*

Marston's short poem is in many ways very unlike the others in this collection. It belongs here by virtue of being an erotic poem based on a story from the *Metamorphoses* (X, 24–97) that is written in a form and style that owe a good deal to *Venus and Adonis*. But it has very little narrative content, no mythological digressions, and almost no references to classical deities or to external events. Rather, it focuses narrowly on the moments when Pygmalion successfully strives to bring the statue of a beautiful woman, which he has carved himself, to life. In short, it exists to realise the male fantasy of arousing an unresponsive woman to sexual desire. Like other poems of this genre, it literally enacts a cliché, but whereas in Lodge or Beaumont this forms only a very minor element in the whole achievement, for Marston's poem this seems to be the *raison d'être*. But the issue of how the poem handles its material is more complex than that. It was published in a single volume entitled *The Metamorphosis of Pygmalion's Image and Certaine Satires*, and in the poem printed next after *The Metamorphosis of Pygmalion's Image*, entitled 'The Authour in prayse of his precedent Poem', the 'author' seems to suggest that *The Metamorphosis* was deliberately written as an exercise in fashionably lascivious verse. As he puts it, it was meant to 'tickle up our lewd Priapians':

> Is not my pen complete? Are not my lines
> Right in the swaggering humour of the times?
> O sing paena to my learned muse.

But is this 'author' Marston himself, or is it his alter ego, the satiric persona 'W. Kinsayder', the pseudonym Marston adopts? (The coined name 'Kinsayder' appears to derive from the now archaic word *kinsing*, meaning to castrate dogs.) And in the context of the whole volume, is *The Metamorphosis of Pygmalion's Image* meant to be read as a parody of Ovidian verse, written by a fictitious poet who is not as accomplished as he thinks he is? This is not the place to deal with these questions, which critics have debated at contentious length; interested readers can follow up the controversy by means of articles cited in the Suggestions for Further Reading[7]. But it is necessary to be alert to the possibility that this poem may not be so much a *part* of the genre of Ovidian verse as it is an implied comment on it. Although the genre was popular and much admired, it also had its detractors and *Venus and Adonis* was regarded by some as the 'true model of a lascivious letcher' (Thomas Freeman, *Epigrams*, 1614), fit reading only for the library of a courtesan. Ironically, the volume in which *The Metamorphosis of Pygmalion's Image* appeared was ordered to be burnt by the ecclesiastical authorities in 1599.

Unlike most Elizabethan epyllia, this poem relates a story of fulfilled love which reverses Ovidian convention, in that the metamorphosis is from a lower to a higher state, from female statue to living woman. It is the antithesis of *Scylle's Metamorphosis* where the woman is punished for her sexual unresponsiveness by being turned to stone. Pygmalion seems initially as if he may be another Narcissistic male enemy to the love of women, like Adonis or Hermaphroditus, for whom the adoration of an image he has himself created stands in for the self-absorption of other lovers. The statue is far more appealing to him than any real woman, and at first he so admires his own 'curious workmanship' that he imagines Ovid himself wishing Corinna might 'show such ivory' when she appeared naked before him (presumably a reference to *Amores*, 1, 5). The theme of the artist in love with his own creation, often treated in paintings of the Pygmalion story, for example, by Jean Leon Gerome, or Pontormo, is suggested by the poem's interior setting. Pygmalion's room or studio represents the enclosed world of the artist (or sexual fantasist), and by the fact that the statue, though given life, remains forever an unnamed image.

But this theme is not all-pervasive. Pygmalion longs for some response to his 'affection's ardour', and he prays to Venus to infuse life into the statue 'that she may equalise affection/And have a mutual love, and love's desire'. Putting his faith in the goddess's power, he gets into bed with the statue and 'a wondrous metamorphosis' occurs. The poem comes to an end as the narrator invites the reader to imagine what he would do at this moment in Pygmalion's place.

Throughout the poem Marston's narrator sustains a teasing relationship with the reader based on a sense of the tension between the imperfect world of real sexual experience inhabited by himself and the (male) reader, and the fantasy world of Pygmalion. The narrator characterises himself as a man condemned like all men to dissatisfaction and frustration on account of the capricious sexual nature of women. The norm for gender relationships in his world is loosely Petrarchan – the man is the ardent wooer, the woman conventionally beautiful, conventionally cold. The narrator invites the reader to share his envy of Pygmalion, for example in his ability to gaze unreproved on the statue's 'parts of secrecy':

> O that my mistress were an image too,
> That I might blameless her perfections view.
> (ll. 65–6)

At the climax of the poem the narrator taunts the reader by appearing to withhold what he knows the reader wants, that is

> The amorous description of that action
> Which Venus seeks, and ever doth require.
> (ll. 196–7)

This is in fact a familiar rhetorical strategy in erotic poetry whereby the poet claims to be incapable of writing sufficiently well or else unwilling to provide some explicit detail, despite achieving the same effect by less obvious means. Marlowe's disclaimer of his poetic ability to treat his subject in appropriately high style in *Hero and Leander* is an example of this ploy:

> I could tell ye
> How smooth his breast was, and how white his belly
> but my rude pen
> Can hardly blazon forth the loves of men,
> Much less of powerful gods.
>
> (ll. 65–72)

In the last stanzas Marston's narrator directs his reader in some detail to use his own sexual imagination, then concludes, echoing Ovid's '*Caetera quid nescit?*' who knows not what ensues? (*Amores* 1, 5). But this coyness only plays at being a retraction at the end of a poem which has acknowledged quite frankly the erotic and titillatory functions of the genre. It is not Ovid as creator of fictions who interests Marston, but how myth, through fantasy, explores human fears and desires.

Modern critics have often termed these epyllia 'ambivalent', in the sense of taking or provoking contradictory emotional attitudes towards a subject (as Ovid did in making Medea say, *'video meliora proboque, deteriora sequor'* – I see and approve what is better, but I follow what is worse (*Metamorphoses* VII, 20–1). The word is particularly appropriate to Marston's poem which seems to indulge and yet also to satirise the narrator's preoccupation with sexual fulfilment. The satiric note is loud in ll. 79–84 where Pygmalion's adoration of the statue is compared to that of 'peevish Papists' crouching before 'some dumb idol', and in ll. 55–60, when the image of a 'subtile City-dame' peeping through her fingers in church conveys a sense of prurience and sexual hypocrisy in relation to the sculptor's inability to refrain from gazing at the statue's private parts. At the end of the poem the reader is both invited to indulge his sexual fantasies and to be reproved for devouring Marston's 'idle poesy' with 'gaping ears'. Elsewhere in the *Pygmalion* volume Marston refers to the poem as 'nastie stuffe . . . maggot-tainted lewd corruption' (*Satyre* VI). The poet's divided attitude towards his material is incorporated into the very texture of the poem. The impulse to satire, never absent from the Elizabethan epyllion, is strongest here.

SANDRA CLARK

References

1. See the articles by P. W. Miller and Walter Allen cited in the Reading list.
2. See L. P. Wilkinson, *Ovid Recalled* (Cambridge, 1955) p. 429.
3. C. S. Lewis, *English Literature in the Sixteenth Century, excluding Drama* (Oxford, 1954), p. 498 and John Buxton, *Elizabethan Taste* (Sussex, 1963, 1983), p. 297. Katherine Duncan-Jones, 'Much Ado with Red and White: The Earliest Readers of Shakespeare's *Venus and Adonis*', *Review of English Studies* XLIV (1993), 479–501 is a good antidote here.
4. For a survey of such readings see Donald G. Watson, 'The Contrarieties of *Venus and Adonis*', *Studies in Philology* 75 (1978), 32–63.
5. J. B. Steane, Marlowe. *A Critical Study* (Cambridge, 1964), p. 332
6. By Ann Thompson in 'Death by Water: The Originality of *Salmacis and Hermaphroditus*', *Modern Language Quarterly* 40 (1979), 99–114.
7. See Adrian Weiss, '"Rhetoric and Satire": New Light on John Marston's *Pygmalion* and the Satires', *The Journal of English and*

Germanic Philology LXXI (1972), 22–35. P. J. Finkelpearl, 'From Petrarch to Ovid: Metamorphoses in John Marston's *The Metamorphoses of Pygmalion's Image*', *English Literary History* 32 (1965), 333–348, is also useful.

NOTE ON THE SELECTION AND TEXTS

The five poems in this selection have been brought together in a modern-spelling edition for the first time. Elizabeth Story Donno included them all, along with several others, in her invaluable old-spelling edition, *Elizabethan Minor Epics* (London, 1963). Those by Lodge, Shakespeare, Marlowe, and Marston were reproduced in *Elizabethan Verse Romances*, edited by M. M. Reese (London, 1968), those by Lodge, Marlowe and Beaumont in *Elizabeth Narrative Verse*, edited by Nigel Alexander (London, 1967). All of these editions, to the frustration of students and teachers, have long been out of print. Whereas *Venus and Adonis* and *Hero and Leander* are relatively easy to obtain, the other texts are not; but for anyone interested in studying the genre as a late-Elizabethan cultural phenomenon it is important to be able to consider a range of examples. The poems have been chosen with regard both to historical significance (as discussed in the introduction) and to literary and erotic quality. Marlowe's *Hero and Leander* has been included without the continuations added after the poet's death by George Chapman (published with Marlowe's poem in one of the two editions of 1598) and Henry Petowe (also 1598). Although unfinished, it is very much a work of art in its own right, and not regularly considered in relation to the continuations. The addition of Chapman's much longer and stylistically dissimilar piece would have unbalanced the selection.

The modern-spelling texts have been taken from M. M. Reese, ed., *Elizabethan Verse Romances* (for Lodge, Shakespeare, Marlowe, and Marston), and from Alexander Dyce, ed., *The Works of Beaumont and Fletcher* (London, 1843–6), vol. 11 (with some slight modifications) for Beaumont. Lodge's *Scylla's Metamorphosis* exists in two early editions, the first of 1589, and the reissue, entitled *Glaucus and Scylla* (1610). All modernised texts of *Venus and Adonis* are based on the first edition of 1593. The text of Marlowe's *Hero and Leander* is based on the first of the two editions of 1598, published by Edward Blount. Dyce based his text of Beaumont's *Salmacis and Hermpahroditus* on the 1640 reprint of the poem by W. W. and Laurence Blaiklocke, *Poems: by Francis Beaumont*, since he was unable to obtain the first edition of 1602. I have compared the texts and made one or two emendations to Dyce's version, which is generally very accurate, to bring it closer to the 1602 text. The text of Marston's *The Metamorphosis of Pygmalion's Image* is based on the edition of 1598. *Amorous Rites* is not a textual edition and notes on variants, where they occur, are not recorded. The modernisation of spelling and punctuation is in accordance with current practice. The glossary is chiefly devoted to the identification of classical names, but also includes a few explanatory notes on other terms. In general, the language of these poems poses few problems for the modern reader, and extensive annotation in an edition of this kind does not seem necessary.

Ceco la bella Dea madre d'Amore   Aura seguendo il suo fatal ardore

Illustration: copyright © The Warburg Institute

AMOROUS RITES

Elizabethan
Erotic Narrative Verse

Thomas Lodge

Scylla's Metamorphosis:
Interlaced with the unfortunate love of Glaucus

(1589)

1

Walking alone (all only full of grief)
Within a thicket near to Isis' flood,
Weeping my wants, and wailing scant relief,
Wringing mine arms (as one with sorrow wood);
 The piteous streams, relenting at my moan,
 Withdrew their tides, and stayed to hear me groan.

2

From forth the channel, with a sorrowing cry
The sea-god Glaucus (with his hallow'd ears
Wet in the tears of his sad mother's dye)
With piteous looks before my face appears;   10
 For whom the nymphs a mossy coat did frame,
 Embroider'd with his Scylla's heavenly name.

3

And as I sat under a willow tree,
The lovely honour of fair Thetis' bower
Repos'd his head upon my faintful knee:
And when my tears had ceas'd their stormy shower
 He dried my cheeks, and then bespake him so,
 As when he wail'd I straight forgot my woe:

4

'Unfortunate, why wand'reth thy content
From forth his scope as wearied of itself?   20
Thy books have school'd thee from this fond repent,
And thou canst talk by proof of wavering pelf:*
     Unto the world such is inconstancy,
     As sap to tree, as apple to the eye.

5

'Mark, how the morn in roseate colour shines,
And straight with clouds the sunny tract is clad;
Then see how pomp through wax and wane declines,
From high to low, from better to the bad:
     Take moist from sea, take colour from his kind,
     Before the world devoid of change thou find.   30

6

'With secret eye look on the earth awhile,
Regard the changes Nature forceth there;
Behold the heavens, whose course all sense beguile;
Respect thyself, and thou shalt find it clear
     That infantlike thou art become a youth,
     And youth forespent, a wretched age ensu'th.

7

'In searching then the schoolmen's cunning notes,
Of heaven, of earth, of flowers, of springing trees,
Of herbs, of metal, and of Thetis' floats,
Of laws and nurture kept among the bees: 40
     Conclude and know times change by course of fate;
     Then mourn no more, but moan my hapless state.'

8

Here gan he pause and shake his heavy head,
And fold his arms, and then unfold them straight;
Fain would he speak, but tongue was charm'd by dread,
Whilst I that saw what woes did him await,
     Comparing his mishaps and moan with mine,
     Gan smile for joy and dry his drooping eyne.

9

But (lo) a wonder; from the channel's glide
A sweet melodious noise of music rose   50
That made the stream to dance a pleasant tide,
The weeds and sallows near the bank that grows
   Gan sing, as when the calmest winds accord
   To greet with balmy breath the fleeting ford.

10

Upon the silver bosom of the stream
First gan fair Themis shake her amber locks,
Whom all the nymphs that wait on Neptune's realm
Attended from the hollow of the rocks.
   In brief, while these rare paragons assemble,
   The wat'ry world to touch their teats do tremble.   60

11

Footing it featly on the grassy ground,
These damsels, circling with their brightsome fairs
The lovesick god and I, about us wound
Like stars that Ariadne's crown repairs:
   Who once hath seen or pride of morn or day,
   Would deem all pomp within their cheeks did play.

12

Nais, fair nymph with Bacchus' ivory touch,
Gan tune a passion with such sweet reports.
And every word, note, sigh, and pause was such,
And every cadence fed with such consorts,   70
   As were the Delian harper* bent to hear,
   Her stately strains might tempt his curious ear.

13

Of love (God wot) the lovely nymph complain'd:
But so of love as forced Love to love her;
And even in love such furious love remain'd,
As searching out his powerful shaft to prove her,
   He found his quiver emptied of the best,
   And felt the arrow sticking in his breast.

14

Under a poplar Themis did repose her,
And from a briar a sweetful branch did pluck: 80
When midst the briar ere she could scarce suppose her
A nightingale gan sing: but woe the luck;
　　The branch so near her breast, while she did quick her
　　To turn her head, on sudden gan to prick her.

15

Whilst smiling Clore, midst her envious blushes,
Gan blame her fear and prettily said thus:
'Worse pricks than these are found among these bushes,
And yet such pricks are scarcely fear'd of us.'
　　'Nay soft (said Chelis), pricks do make birds sing,
　　But pricks in ladies' bosoms often sting.'   90

16

Thus jest they on the nightingale's report,
And on the prickle of the eglantine,
On Nais' song, and all the whole consort
In public this sweet sentence did assign:
　　That while some smile, some sigh through change of time;
　　Some smart, some sport, amidst their youthly prime.

17

Such wreaths as bound the Theban's* ivory brow,
Such gay-trick'd garlands plait these jolly dames;
The flowers themselves, when as the nymphs gan vow,
Gan vail their crests in honour of their names: 100
　　And smil'd their sweet and woo'd with so much glee,
　　As if they said, 'Sweet nymph, come gather me.'

18

But pensive Glaucus, passionate with painings,
Amidst their revel thus began his ruth:
'Nymphs, fly these groves late blasted with my plainings,
For cruel Scylla nill regard my truth:
　　And leave us two consorted in our groanings,
　　To register with tears our bitter moanings.

19

'The floods do fail their course to see our cross,
The fields forsake their green to hear our grief, 110
The rocks will weep whole springs to mark our loss,
The hills relent to store our scant relief,
   The air repines, the pensive birds are heavy,
   The trees to see us pain'd no more are leafy.

20

'Ay me, the shepherds let their flocks want feeding,
And flocks to see their paly face are sorry;
The nymphs to spy the flocks and shepherds needing,
Prepare their tears to hear our tragic story:
   Whil'st we, surpris'd with grief, cannot disclose them,
   With sighing wish the world for to suppose them. 120

21

'He that hath seen the sweet Arcadian boy*
Wiping the purple from his forced wound,
His pretty tears betokening his annoy,
His sighs, his cries, his falling on the ground,
   The echoes ringing from the rocks his fall,
   The trees with tears reporting of his thrall:

22

'And Venus starting at her love-mate's cry,
Forcing her birds to haste her chariot on;
And full of grief at last with piteous eye
Seeing where all pale with death he lay alone, 130
   Whose beauty quail'd, as wont the lilies droop
   When wasteful winter winds do make them stoop:

23

'Her dainty hand address'd to daw her dear,
Her roseal lip allied to his pale cheek,
Her sighs, and then her looks and heavy cheer,
Her bitter threats, and then her passions meek;
   How on his senseless corpse she lay a-crying,
   As if the boy were then but new a-dying.

24

'He that hath view'd Angelica the fair
Bestraught with fancy near the Caspian springs,   140
Renting the tresses of her golden hair;
How on her harp with piteous notes she sings
   Of Roland's ruth, of Medor's false depart,
   Sighing each rest from centre of her heart;

25

'How now she writes upon a beechen bough
Her Medor's name, and bedlam-like again
Calls all the heaven to witness of his vow
And straight again begins a mournful strain,
   And how in thought of her true faith forsooken
   He fled her bowers, and how his league was broken.   150

26

'Ay me, who marks her harp hang up again
Upon the willows water'd with her tears,
And how she rues to read her Roland's pain,
When but the shadow of his name appears,
   Would make more plainings from his eyes to flee
   Than tears distil from amber-weeping tree.

27

'He that hath known the passionate mishaps
That near Olympus fair Lucina felt
When as her Latmian love* her fancy traps,
How with suspect her inward soul doth melt;   160
   Or mark'd the morn her Cephalus complaining;
   May then recount the course of all our paining.

28

'But tender nymphs, to you belongs no teen;
Then favour me in flying from this bower
Whereas but care and thought of crosses been;
Leave me, that lose myself through fancy's power;
   Through fancy's power, which had I leave to lose it,
   No fancy then should see me for to choose it.

29

'When you are fled, the heaven shall lour for sorrow,
The day o'ercast shall be betime with sable,   170
The air from sea such streaming showers shall borrow
As earth to bear the brunt shall not be able,
   And ships shall safely sail whereas beforn
   The ploughman watch'd the reaping of his corn.

30

'Go you in peace to Neptune's wat'ry sound;
No more may Glaucus play him with so pretty,
But shun resort where solace nill be found,
And plain my Scylla's pride and want of pity:
   Alas sweet nymphs, my godhead's all in vain,
   For why this breast includes immortal pain.   180

31

'Scylla hath eyes, but too sweet eyes hath Scylla;
Scylla hath hands, fair hands, but coy in touching;
Scylla in wit surpasseth grave Sibylla;
Scylla hath words, but words well stor'd with grutching;
   Scylla a saint in look, no saints in scorning:
   Look saint-like, Scylla, lest I die with mourning.

32

'Alas, why talk I? Sea-god, cease to mourn her,
For in her nay my joys are ever ceasing:
Cease life or love, then shall I never blame her;
But neither love nor life may find decreasing.   190
   A mortal wound is my immortal being,
   Which passeth thought, or eyes' advised seeing.'

33

Herewith his falt'ring tongue, by sighs oppress'd,
Forsook his office, and his blood resorted
To feed the heart that wholly was distress'd,
Whilst pale (like Pallas' flower)* my knees supported
   His feeble head and arm, so full of anguish,
   That they which saw his sorrows gan to languish.

34

Themis, the coyest of this beauteous train,
On hilly tops the wond'rous moly* found,   200
Which dipp'd in balmy dew she gan to strain,
And brought her present to recure his wound:
  Clore she gathered Amaranthus' flower,
  And Nais Ajax' blossom* in that stour.

35

Some chafe his temples with their lovely hands,
Some sprinkle water on his pale wan cheeks,
Some weep, some wake, some curse affection's bands,
To see so young, so fair, become so weak:
  But not their piteous herbs or springs have working
  To ease that heart where wanton love is lurking.   210

36

Natheless, though loth to show his holy kindness,
On every one he spent a look for favour,
And pray'd their pardon, vouching Cupid's blindness,
(Oh, fancies fond that naught but sorrows savour);
  To see a lovely god leave sea nymphs so,
  Who cannot doom upon his deadly woe?

37

Themis, that knew that waters long restrain'd
Break forth with greater billows than the brooks
That sweetly float through meads with flowers distain'd,
With cheerful lays did raise his heavy looks,   220
  And bade him speak and tell what him aggriev'd:
  For griefs disclos'd (said she) are soon reliev'd.

38

And as she wish'd, so all the rest did woo him;
By whose incessant suits at last invited,
He thus discover'd that which did undo him,
And orderly his hideous harms recited,
  When first with finger's wag he gan to still them,
  And thus with dreary terms of love did fill them.

39

'Ah nymphs,' (quoth he), 'had I by reason learnt
That secret art which birds have gain'd by sense,   230
By due foresight misfortune to prevent;
Or could my wit control mine eyes' offence;
   You then should smile, and I should tell such stories
   As woods and waves should triumph in our glories.

40

'But Nereus'* daughters, sea-borne saints, attend:
Lake-breeding geese, when from the eastern clime
They list unto the western waters wend
To choose their place of rest by course of time,
   Approaching Taurus' haughty-topped hill
   They charm their cackle by this wondrous skill.   240

41

'The climbing mountain, neighbouring air well-nigh,
Hath harbour'd in his rocks and desert haunts
Whole eeries of eagles, prest to fly,
That gazing on the sun their birthright vaunts;
   Which birds of Jove with deadly feud pursue
   The wandering geese, when so they press in view.

42

'These fearful flitting troops, by Nature taught,
Passing these dangerous places of pursuit,
When all the desert vales they through have sought,
With pebbles stop their beaks to make them mute,*   250
   And by this means their dangerous deaths prevent
   And gain their wished waters of frequent.

43

'But I, fond God, I god complain thy folly;
Let birds by sense exceed my reason far:
Whilom than I who was more strong and jolly,
Who more contemn'd affection's wanton war?
   Who less than I lov'd lustful Cupid's arrows,
   Who now with curse and plague poor Glaucus harrows?

44

'How have I leapt to hear the Tritons play
A harsh retreat unto the swelling floods?   260
How have I kept the dolphins at a bay,
When as I meant to charm their wanton moods?
  How have the angry winds grown calm for love,
  When as these fingers did my harp strings move?

45

'Was any nymph, you nymphs, was ever any
That tangled not her fingers in my tress?
Some well I wot, and of that some full many,
Wish'd or my fair or their desire were less:
  Even Ariadne, gazing from the sky,
Became enamour'd of poor Glaucus' eye.   270

46

'Amidst this pride of youth and beauty's treasure
It was my chance, you floods can tell my chancing,
Fleeting along Sicilian bounds for pleasure,
To spy a nymph of such a radiant glancing,
  As when I look'd, a beam of subtil firing
  From eye to heart incens'd a deep desiring.

47

'Ah, had the veil of reason clad mine eye,
This foe of freedom had not burnt my heart:
But birds are blest, and most accurs'd am I
Who must report her glories to my smart: 280
  The nymph I saw and lov'd her, all too cruel,
  Scylla, fair Scylla, my fond fancy's jewel.

48

'Her hair not truss'd but scatter'd on her brow,
Surpassing Hybla's* honey for the view,
Or soften'd golden wires; I know not how
Love with a radiant beauty did pursue
  My too judicial eyes, in darting fire
  That kindled straight in me my fond desire.

49

'Within these snares first was my heart entrapp'd,
Till through those golden shrouds mine eyes did see   290
An ivory-shadow'd front, wherein was wrapp'd
Those pretty bowers where graces couched be:
  Next which her cheeks appear'd like crimson silk,
  Or ruddy rose bespread on whitest milk.

50

'Twixt which the nose in lovely tenor bends,
(Too traitorous pretty for a lover's view):
Next which her lips like violets commends
By true proportion that which doth ensue;
  Which when they smile present unto the eyes
  The ocean's pride and ivory paradise.   300

51

'Her polish'd neck of milk-white snows doth shine,
As when the moon in winter night beholds them:
Her breast of alabaster clear and fine,
Whereon two rising apples fair unfolds them,
  Like Cynthia's face when in her full she shineth,
  And blushing to her love-mate's bower declineth.

52

'From whence in length her arms do sweetly spread
Like two rare branchy saples in the spring,
Yielding five lovely sprigs from every head,
Proportion'd alike in everything;   310
  Which featly sprout in length like spring-born friends,
  Whose pretty tops with five sweet roses ends.

53

'But why, alas, should I that marble hide
That doth adorn the one and other flank,
From whence a mount of quicken'd snow doth glide;
Or else the vale that bounds this milk-white bank,
  Where Venus and her sisters hide the fount
  Whose lovely nectar doth all sweets surmount.

54

'Confounded with descriptions, I must leave them;
Lovers must think, and poets must report them: 320
For silly wits may never well conceive them,
Unless a special grace from heaven consort them.
    Aye's me, these fairs attending Scylla won me:
    But now (sweet nymphs) attend what hath undone me.

55

'The lovely breast where all this beauty rested
Shrouded within a world of deep disdain:
For where I thought my fancy should be feasted
With kind affect, alas (unto my pain)
    When first I wooed, the wanton straight was flying,
    And gave repulse before we talk'd of trying.   330

56

'How oft have I (too often have I done so)
In silent night when every eye was sleeping,
Drawn near her cave, in hope her love were won so,
Forcing the neighbouring waters through my weeping
    To wake the winds, who did afflict her dwelling
    Whilst I with tears my passion was a-telling.

57

'When midst the Caspian seas the wanton play'd
I drew whole wreaths of coral from the rocks
And in her lap my heavenly presents laid:
But she unkind rewarded me with mocks;   340
    Such are the fruits that spring from ladies' coying,
    Who smile at tears and are entrapp'd with toying.

58

'Tongue might grow weary to report my wooings,
And heart might burst to think of her denial:
May none be blam'd but heaven for all these doings,
That yield no helps in midst of all my trial.
    Heart, tongue, thought, pen nill serve me to repent me;
    Disdain herself should strive for to lament me:

59

'Wretched Love, let me die, end my love by my death;
Dead, alas I live. Fly, my life! fade, my love!   350
Out, alas, love abides, still I 'joy vital breath:
Death is love, love is death: woe is me that do prove.
  Pain and woe, care and grief every day about me hovers:
  Then but death what can quell all the plagues of hapless lovers?

60

'Ay me, my moanings are like water drops
That need an age to pierce her marble heart;
I sow'd true zeal, yet fruitless were my crops:
I plighted faith, yet falsehood wrought my smart:
  I prais'd her looks, her looks despised Glaucus;
  Was ever amorous sea-god scorned thus?   360

61

'A hundred swelling tides my mother spent
Upon these locks, and all her nymphs were prest
To pleat them fair when to her bower I went:
He that hath seen the wand'ring Phoebus' crest
  Touch'd with the crystal of Eurotas' spring,
  The pride of these my bushy locks might sing.

62

'But short discourse beseems my bad success.
Each office of a lover I perform'd:
So fervently my passions did her press,
So sweet my lays, my speech so well reform'd,   370
  That (cruel) when she saw naught would beguile me,
  With angry looks the nymph did thus exile me:

63

' "Pack hence, thou fondling, to the western seas,
Within some calmy river shroud thy head:
For never shall my fair thy love appease,
Since fancy from this bosom late is fled:
  And if thou love me, show it in departing:
  For why thy presence doth procure my smarting."

64

'This said, with angry looks away she hasted
As fast as fly the floods before the winds: 380
When I (poor soul), with wretched sorrows wasted,
Exclaim'd on love, which wit and reason blinds:
    And banish'd from her bower, with woeful posting
    I bent myself to seek a foreign coasting.

65

'At last in wand'ring through the greater seas
It was my chance to pass the noted straits:
And wearied sore in seeking after ease,
Amidst the creeks, and wat'ry cool receipts,
    I spied from far, by help of sunny beams,
    A fruitful isle begirt with ocean streams.   390

66

'Westward I fleeted, and with heedful eye
Beheld the chalky cliffs that tempt the air,
Till at the last it was my chance to spy
A pleasant entrance to the floods' repair;
    Through which I press'd, and wond'ring there beheld
    On either side a sweet and fruitful field.

67

'Isis (the lady of that lovely stream)
Made a holiday in view of my resort;
And all the nymphs of that her wat'ry realm
Gan trip for joy, to make me mickle sport: 400
    But I (poor soul) with no such joys contented,
    Forsook the bowers, and secretly lamented.

68

'All solitary roam I hereabout,
Now on the shore, now in the stream I weep;
Fire burns within, and ghastly fear without,
No rest, no ease, no hope of any sleep:
    Poor banish'd god, here have I still remain'd,
    Since time my Scylla hath my suits disdain'd.

69

'And here consort I now with hapless men,
Yielding them comfort, though my wound be cureless.   410
Songs of remorse I warble now and then,
Wherein I curse fond Love and Fortune dureless;
   Wanhope my weal, my trust but bad adventure,
   Circumference is care, my heart the centre.'

70

Whilst thus he spake, fierce Ate charm'd his tongue,
His senses fail'd, his arms were folded straight,
And now he sighs, and then his heart is stung;
Again he speaks 'gainst fancy's fond deceit,
   And tears his tresses with his fingers fair,
   And rents his robes, half-mad with deep despair.   420

71

The piteous nymphs that view'd his heavy plight,
And heard the sequel of his bad success,
Did loose the springs of their remorseful sight,
And wept so sore to see his scant redress
   That of their tears there grew a pretty brook,
   Whose crystals clear the clouds of pensive look.

72

Alas, woe's me, how oft have I beswept
So fair, so young, so lovely, and so kind;
And whilst the god upon my bosom slept,
Beheld the scars of his afflicted mind,   430
   Imprinted in his ivory brow by care
   That fruitless fancy left unto his share.

73

My wand'ring lines, bewitch not so my senses:
But, gentle Muse, direct their course aright;
Delays in tragic tales procure offences:
Yield me such feeling words that whilst I write
   My working lines may fill mine eyes with languish,
   And they to note my moans may melt with anguish.

74

The woeful Glaucus, thus with woes attainted,
The pensive nymphs aggriev'd to see his plight,   440
The floods and fields with his laments acquainted,
Myself amaz'd to see this heavy sight;
   On sudden, Thetis with her train approach'd,
   And gravely thus her amorous son reproach'd:

75

'My son (said she), immortal have I made thee;
Amidst my wat'ry realms who may compare
Or match thy might? Why then should care invade thee,
That art so young, so lovely, fresh and fair?
   Alas, fond god, it merits great reproving
   In states of worth to dote on foolish loving.   450

76

'Come, wend with me, and midst thy father's bower
Let us disport and frolic for a while
In spite of love: although he pout and lour,
Good exercise will idle lusts beguile:
   Let wanton Scylla coy her where she will,
   Live thou, my son, by reason's level still.'

77

Thus said the goddess: and although her words
Gave signs of counsel, pomp and majesty,
Yet natheless her piteous eye affords
Some pretty witness to the standers-by   460
   That in her thoughts (for all her outward show)
   She mourn'd to see her son amated so.

78

But (welladay) her words have little force;
That hapless lover, worn with working woe,
Upon the ground lay pale as any corse,
And were not tears which from his eyes did flow,
   And sighs that witness he enjoy'd his breath,
   They might have thought him citizen of Death.

79

Which spectacle of care made Thetis bow,
And call on Glaucus, and command her son   470
To yield her right, and her advice allow.
But (woe) the man whom fancy had undone
    Nill mark her rules: nor words nor weeping tears
    Can fasten counsel in the lover's ears.

80

The Queen of Sea,* with all her nymphs assur'd
That no persuasion might relieve his care,
Kneeling adown, their falt'ring tongues enur'd
To tempt fair Venus by their vowed prayer:
    The course whereof, as I could bear in mind,
    With sorrowing sobs they utter'd in this kind: 480

81

'Born of the sea, thou Paphian Queen of Love,*
Mistress of sweet conspiring harmony:
Lady of Cyprus, for whose sweet behove
The shepherds praise the youth of Thessaly:
    Daughter of Jove and sister to the Sun,
    Assist poor Glaucus, late by love undone.

82

'So mayst thou bain thee in th' Arcadian brooks,
And play with Vulcan's rival when thou list,
And calm his jealous anger by thy looks,
And knit thy temples with a roseate twist,   490
    If thou thyself and thine almighty son
    Assist poor Glaucus, late by love undone.

83

'May earth still praise thee for her kind increase,
And beasts adore thee for their fruitful wombs,
And fowls with notes thy praises never cease,
And bees admire thee for their honeycombs:
    So thou thyself and thine almighty son
    Assist poor Glaucus, late by love undone.'

84

No sooner from her reverent lips were past
Those latter lines but, mounting in the east,   500
Fair Venus in her ivory coach did haste,
And toward those pensive dames her course address'd;
    Her doves so plied their waving wings with flight
    That straight the sacred goddess came in sight.

85

Upon her head she bare that gorgeous crown
Wherein the poor Amyntas is a star;
Her lovely locks her bosom hung adown
(Those nets that first ensnar'd the God of War):
    Delicious lovely shine her pretty eyes,
    And on her cheeks carnation clouds arise;   510

86

The stately robe she ware upon her back
Was lily-white, wherein with coloured silk
Her nymphs had blaz'd the young Adonis' wrack,
And Leda's rape by swan as white as milk,
    And on her lap her lovely son* was plac'd,
    Whose beauty all his mother's pomp defac'd.

87

A wreath of roses hemm'd his temples in,
His tress was curl'd and clear as beaten gold;
Haught were his looks, and lovely was his skin,
Each part as pure as heaven's eternal mould,   520
    And on his eyes a milk-white wreath was spread,
    Which 'longst his back with pretty plaits did shed.

88

Two dainty wings of parti-coloured plumes
Adorn his shoulders, dallying with the wind;
His left hand wields a torch that ever fumes:
And in his right, his bow that fancies bind,
    And on his back, his quiver hangs, well stor'd
    With sundry shafts that sundry hearts have gor'd.

89

The deities arriv'd in place desir'd,
Fair Venus her to Thetis first bespake: 530
'Princess of Sea' (quoth she), 'as you requir'd,
From Sestos with my son my course I take:
  Frolic, fair goddess, nymphs forsake your plaining,
  My son hath power and favour yet remaining.'

90

With that the reverend powers each other kiss'd,
And Cupid smil'd upon the nymphs for pleasure:
So naught but Glaucus' solace there was miss'd:
Which to effect the nymphs withouten measure
  Entreat the god, who at the last drew nigh
  The place where Glaucus full of care did lie; 540

91

And from his bow a furious dart he sent
Into that wound which he had made before:
That like Achilles' sword became the taint
To cure the wound that it had carv'd before:
  And suddenly the sea-god started up,
  Reviv'd, reliev'd, and free from fancy's cup.

92

No more of love, no more of hate he spoke,
No more he forc'd the sighs from out his breast:
His sudden joy his pleasing smiles provoke,
And all aloft he shakes his bushy crest, 550
  Greeting the gods and goddesses beside,
  And every nymph upon that happy tide.

93

Cupid and he together, hand in hand,
Approach the place of this renowned train:
'Ladies' (said he), 'releas'd from amorous band,
Receive my prisoner to your grace again.'
  Glaucus gave thanks, when Thetis, glad with bliss,
  Embrac'd his neck and his kind cheeks did kiss.

94

To see the nymphs in flocks about him play,
How Nais kempt his head, and wash'd his brows: 560
How Thetis check'd him with his welladay,
How Clore told him of his amorous vows,
   How Venus prais'd him for his faithful love,
   Within my heart a sudden joy did move.

95

Whilst in this glee this holy troop delight,
Along the stream afar fair Scylla floated,
And coyly vaunts her crest in open sight:
Whose beauties all the tides with wonder noted,
   'Fore whom Palemon and the Tritons danc'd
   Whilst she her limbs upon the tide advanc'd: 570

96

Whose swift approach made all the godheads wonder:
Glaucus gan smile to see his lovely foe,
Rage almost rent poor Thetis' heart asunder:
Was never happy troop confused so
   As were these deities and dainty dames,
   When they beheld the cause of Glaucus' blames.

97

Venus commends the carriage of her eye,
Nais upbraids the dimple in her chin,
Cupid desires to touch the wanton's thigh,
Clore she swears that every eye doth sin   580
   That likes a nymph that so contemneth love
   As no attempts her lawless heart may move.

98

Thetis, impatient of her wrong sustain'd,
With envious tears her roseate cheeks afflicted,
And thus of Scylla's former pride complain'd;
'Cupid' (said she) 'see her that hath inflicted
   The deadly wound that harm'd my lovely son,
   From whom the offspring of my care begun.

99

'Oh, if there dwell within my breast, my boy,
Or grace, or pity, or remorse (said she),   5!
Now bend thy bow, abate yon wanton's joy,
And let these nymphs thy rightful justice see.'
 The god, soon won, gan shoot, and cleft her heart
 With such a shaft as caus'd her endless smart.

100

The tender nymph, attainted unawares,
Fares like the Libyan lioness that flies
The hunter's lance that wounds her in his snares;
Now gins she love, and straight on Glaucus cries;
 Whilst on the shore the goddesses rejoice,
 And all the nymphs afflict the air with noise.   600

101

To shore she flits, and swift as Afric wind
Her footing glides upon the yielding grass,
And wounded by affect, recure to find
She suddenly with sights approach'd the place
 Where Glaucus sat, and weary with her harms
 Gan clasp the sea-god in her amorous arms.

102

'Glaucus, my love' (quoth she), 'look on thy lover,
Smile, gentle Glaucus, on the nymph that likes thee.'
But stark as stone sat he, and list not prove her:
Ah, silly nymph, the selfsame god that strikes thee   610
 With fancy's dart, and hath thy freedom slain,
 Wounds Glaucus with the arrow of disdain.

103

Oh, kiss no more, kind nymph, he likes no kindness,
Love sleeps in him, to flame within thy breast;
Clear'd are his eyes, where thine are clad with blindness;
Freed be his thoughts, where thine must taste unrest:
 Yet nill she leave, for never love will leave her,
 But fruitless hopes and fatal haps deceive her.

104

Lord, how her lips do dwell upon his cheeks;
And how she looks for babies in his eyes: 620
And how she sighs, and swears she loves and leeks,
And how she vows, and he her vows envies:
   Trust me, the envious nymphs, in looking on,
   Were forc'd with tears for to assist her moan.

105

How oft with blushes would she plead for grace,
How oft with whisperings would she tempt his ears:
How oft with crystal did she wet his face:
How oft she wip'd them with her amber hairs:
   So oft, methought, I oft in heart desir'd
   To see the end whereto Disdain aspir'd.   630

106

Palemon with the Tritons roar for grief,
To see the mistress of their joys amated:
But Glaucus scorns the nymph, that waits relief:
And more she loves, the more the sea-god hated;
   Such change, such chance, such suits, such storms, believe me,
   Poor silly wretch, did heartily aggrieve me.

107

As when the fatal bird of augury,*
Seeing a stormy dismal cloud arise
Within the south, foretells with piteous cry
The weeping tempest that on sudden hies: 640
   So she, poor soul, in view of his disdain
   Began to descant on her future pain.

108

And fixing eye upon the fatal ground,
Whole hosts of floods drew dew from out her eyes;
And when through inward grief the lass did sound,
The soften'd grass like billows did arise
   To woo her breasts, and wed her limbs so dainty,
   Whom wretched love had made so weak and fainty.

109

Aye's me, methinks I see here Thetis' fingers
Renting her locks as she were woe-begone her;   650
And now her lips upon his lipping, lingers:
Oh, ling'ring pain, where love nill list to moan her:
 Rue me that writes, for why her ruth deserves it:
 Hope needs must fail, where sorrow scarce preserves it.

110

To make long tale were tedious to the woeful,
Woeful that read what woeful she approved:
In brief her heart with deep despair was full,
As since she might not win her sweet beloved,
 With hideous cries like wind born back, she fled
 Unto the sea, and toward Sicilia sped.   660

111

Sweet Zephyrus upon that fatal hour
In hapless tide midst wat'ry world was walking;
Whose milder sighs, alas, had little power
To whisper peace amongst the godheads talking:
 Who all in one conclude for to pursue
 The hapless nymph, to see what would ensue.

112

Venus herself and her fair son gan hie
Within their ivory coach, drawn forth by doves,
After this hapless nymph, their power to try:
The nymphs, in hope to see their vowed loves,   670
 Gan cut the wat'ry bosom of the tide,
 As in Caÿster Phoebus' birds do glide.

113

Thetis in pomp upon a Triton's back
Did post her straight, attended by her train;
But Glaucus, free from love by lovers' wrack,
Seeing me pensive where I did remain,
 Upon a dolphin hors'd me as he was;
 Thus on the ocean hand in hand we pass.

114

Our talk midway was nought but still of wonder,
Of change, of chance, of sorrow, and her ending;   680
I wept for want: he said, 'Time brings men under,
And secret want can find but small befriending.'
    And as he said, in that before I tried it,
    I blam'd my wit forewarn'd, yet never spied it.

115

What need I talk the order of my way
(Discourse was steersman while my bark did sail,
My ship conceit, and fancy was my bay:
If these fail me, then faint, my muse, and fail)
    Hast brought us where the hapless nymph sojourn'd,
    Beating the weeping waves that for her mourn'd?   690

116

He that hath seen the northern blasts despoil
The pomp of prime, and with a whistling breath
Blast and disperse the beauties of the soil,
May think upon her pains more worse than death.
    Alas, poor lass, the echoes in the rocks
    Of Sicily her piteous planning mocks.

117

Echo herself, when Scylla cried out, 'O love,'
With piteous voice from out her hollow den
Return'd these words, these words of sorrow, *'No love'*.
'No love (quoth she), then fie on traitorous men,   700
    Then fie on hope: *'Then fie on hope* (quoth Echo).
    To every word the nymph did answer so.

118

For every sigh, the rocks return a sigh;
For every tear, the fountains yield a drop;
Till we at last the place approached nigh,
And heard the nymph that fed on sorrow's sop
    Make woods, and waves, and rocks, and hills admire
    The wondrous force of her untam'd desire.

119

'Glaucus (quoth she) is fair:' whilst Echo sings
Glaucus is fair: 'But yet he hateth Scylla',   710
The wretch reports: and then her arms she wrings
Whilst Echo tells her this: *He hateth Scylla*,
    'No hope (quoth she): *No hope* (quoth Echo) then.
    Then *fie on men*: when she said, 'Fie on men.'

120

Fury and Rage, Wanhope, Despair, and Woe,
From Ditis' den by Ate sent, drew nigh:
Fury was red, with rage his eyes did glow,
Whole flakes of fire from forth his mouth did fly,
    His hands and arms ibath'd in blood of those
    Whom fortune, sin, or fate made country's foes.   720

121

Rage, wan and pale, upon a tiger sat,
Gnawing upon the bones of mangled men;
Naught can he view, but he repin'd thereat:
His locks were snakes bred forth in Stygian den;
    Next whom, Despair, that deep-disdained elf,
    Delightless liv'd, still stabbing of herself.

122

Woe, all in black, within her hands did bear
The fatal torches of a funeral;
Her cheeks were wet, dispersed was her hair,
Her voice was shrill (yet loathsome therewithal):   730
    Wanhope (poor soul) on broken anchor sits,
    Wringing his arms as robbed of his wits.

123

These five at once the sorrowing nymph assail,
And captive lead her bound into the rocks,
Where howling still she strives for to prevail;
With no avail yet strives she: for her locks
    Are chang'd with wonder into hideous sands,
    And hard as flint become her snow-white hands.

124

The waters howl with fatal tunes about her,
The air doth scout when as she turns within them,   740
The winds and waves with puffs and billows scout her;
Waves storm, air scouts, both wind and waves begin them
  To make the place this mournful nymph doth weep in
  A hapless haunt whereas no nymph may keep in.

125

The seaman, wand'ring by that famous isle,
Shuns all with fear, dispairing Scylla's bower;
Nymphs, sea-gods, sirens, when they list to smile
Forsake the haunt of Scylla in that stour:
  Ah, nymphs, thought I, if every coy one felt
  The like mishaps, their flinty hearts would melt.   750

126

Thetis rejoic'd to see her foe depress'd,
Glaucus was glad, since Scylla was enthrall'd;
The nymphs gan smile, to boast their Glaucus' rest:
Venus and Cupid, in their thrones install'd,
  At Thetis' beck to Neptune's bower repair,
  Whereas they feast amidst his palace fair.

127

Of pure immortal nectar is their drink,
And sweet ambrosia dainty do repast them,
The Tritons sing, Palemon smiles to think
Upon the chance, and all the nymphs do haste them   760
  To trick up mossy garlands where they woon,
  For lovely Venus and her conquering son.

128

From forth the fountains of his mother's store,
Glaucus let fly a dainty crystal bain
That wash'd the nymphs, with labour tir'd before:
Cupid he trips among this lovely train;
  Alonely* I apart did write this story
  With many a sigh and heart full sad and sorry.

129

Glaucus, when all the goddesses took rest,
Mounted upon a dolphin full of glee: 770
Convey'd me friendly from this honour'd feast,
And by the way, such sonnets sang to me,
   That all the dolphins neighbouring of his glide
   Danc'd with delight, his reverend course beside.

130

At last he left me where at first he found me,
Willing me let the world and ladies know
Of Scylla's pride; and then by oath he bound me
To write no more of that whence shame doth grow:
   Or tie my pen to penny-knaves' delight,
   But live with fame and so for fame to write.   780

Envoy

Ladies, he left me, trust me I missay not,
But so he left me as he will'd me tell you,
That nymphs must yield, when faithful lovers stray not,
Lest through contempt almighty love compel you
   With Scylla in the rocks to make your biding,
   A cursed plague, for women's proud back-sliding.

William Shakespeare

Venus and Adonis

(1593)

1

Even as the sun with purple-colour'd face
Had ta'en his last leave of the weeping morn,
Rose-cheek'd Adonis hied him to the chase,
Hunting he lov'd, but love he laugh'd to scorn:
   Sick-thoughted Venus makes amain unto him,
   And like a bold-fac'd suitor 'gins to woo him.

2

'Thrice fairer than myself, (thus she began)
The field's chief flower, sweet above compare,
Stain to all nymphs, more lovely than a man,
More white, and red, than doves or roses are: 10
   Nature that made thee with herself at strife
   Saith that the world hath ending with thy life.

3

'Vouchsafe, thou wonder, to alight thy steed,
And rein his proud head to the saddle bow;
If thou wilt deign this favour, for thy meed
A thousand honey secrets shalt thou know:
   Here come and sit, where never serpent hisses,
   And being set, I'll smother thee with kisses.

4

'And yet not cloy thy lips with loath'd satiety,
But rather famish them amid their plenty,   20
Making them red, and pale, with fresh variety:
Ten kisses short as one, one long as twenty:
   A summer's day will seem an hour but short,
   Being wasted in such time-beguiling sport.'

5

With this she seizeth on his sweating palm,
The precedent of pith and livelihood,
And, trembling in her passion, calls it balm,
Earth's sovereign salve to do a goddess good.
    Being so enrag'd, desire doth lend her force
    Courageously to pluck him from his horse.   30

6

Over one arm the lusty courser's rein,
Under her other was the tender boy,
Who blush'd and pouted in a dull disdain,
With leaden appetite, unapt to toy;
    She red and hot as coals of glowing fire,
    He red for shame, but frosty in desire.

7

The studded bridle in a ragged bough
Nimbly she fastens, (oh, how quick is love!)
The steed is stalled up, and even now
To tie the rider she begins to prove: 40
    Backward she push'd him, as she would be thrust,
    And govern'd him in strength though not in lust.

8

So soon was she along as he was down,
Each leaning on their elbows and their hips:
Now doth she stroke his cheek, now doth he frown,
And 'gins to chide, but soon she stops his lips,
    And kissing speaks, with lustful language broken,
    'If thou wilt chide, thy lips shall never open.'

9

He burns with bashful shame, she with her tears
Doth quench the maiden burning of his cheeks;   50
Then with her windy sighs and golden hairs
To fan and blow them dry again she seeks.
    He saith, she is immodest, blames her miss;
    What follows more she murders with a kiss.

10

Even as an empty eagle, sharp by fast,
Tires with her beak on feathers, flesh, and bone,
Shaking her wings, devouring all in haste,
Till either gorge be stuff'd, or prey be gone:
   Even so she kiss'd his brow, his cheek, his chin,
   And where she ends, she doth anew begin.   60

11

Forc'd to content, but never to obey,
Panting he lies, and breatheth in her face.
She feedeth on the steam as on a prey,
And calls it heavenly moisture, air of grace,
   Wishing her cheeks were gardens full of flowers,
   So they were dew'd with such distilling showers.

12

Look how a bird lies tangled in a net,
So fasten'd in her arms Adonis lies;
Pure shame and aw'd resistance made him fret,
Which bred more beauty in his angry eyes: 70
   Rain added to a river that is rank
   Perforce will force it overflow the bank.

13

Still she entreats, and prettily entreats,
For to a pretty ear she tunes her tale.
Still is he sullen, still he lours and frets,
'Twixt crimson shame and anger ashy pale;
   Being red she loves him best, and being white,
   Her best is better'd with a more delight.

14

Look how he can, she cannot choose but love,
And by her fair immortal hand she swears   80
From his soft bosom never to remove,
Till he take truce with her contending tears,
   Which long have rain'd, making her cheeks all wet,
   And one sweet kiss shall pay this countless debt.

15

Upon this promise did he raise his chin,
Like a divedapper peering through a wave,
Who, being look'd on, ducks as quickly in:
So offers he to give what she did crave;
   But when her lips were ready for his pay,
   He winks, and turns his lips another way.   90

16

Never did passenger in summer's heat
More thirst for drink than she for this good turn.
Her help she sees, but help she cannot get;
She bathes in water, yet her fire must burn:
   'Oh pity,' gan she cry, 'flint-hearted boy,
   'Tis but a kiss I beg, why art thou coy?'

17

'I have been woo'd, as I entreat thee now,
Even by the stern and direful god of war,
Whose sinewy neck in battle ne'er did bow,
Who conquers where he comes in every jar;   100
   Yet hath he been my captive and my slave,
   And begg'd for that which thou unask'd shalt have.

18

'Over my altars hath he hung his lance,
His batter'd shield, his uncontrolled crest,
And for my sake hath learn'd to sport and dance,
To toy, to wanton, dally, smile and jest,
   Scorning his churlish drum and ensign red,
   Making my arms his field, his tent my bed.

19

'Thus he that over-rul'd I over-sway'd,
Leading him prisoner in a red-rose chain;   110
Strong-temper'd steel his stronger strength obey'd.
Yet was he servile to my coy disdain.
   Oh, be not proud, nor brag not of thy might,
   For mast'ring her that foil'd the god of fight!

20

'Touch but my lips with those fair lips of thine —
Though mine be not so fair, yet are they red —
The kiss shall be thine own as well as mine.
What see'st thou in the ground? hold up thy head,
　Look in mine eyeballs, there thy beauty lies;
　Then why not lips on lips, since eyes in eyes?   120

21

'Art thou asham'd to kiss? then wink again,
And I will wink; so shall the day seem night.
Love keeps his revels where there are but twain:
Be bold to play, our sport is not in sight.
　These blue-vein'd violets whereon we lean
　Never can blab, nor know not what we mean.

22

'The tender spring upon thy tempting lip
Shews thee unripe; yet mayst thou well be tasted;
Make use of time, let not advantage slip;
Beauty within itself should not be wasted;   130
　Fair flowers that are not gather'd in their prime
　Rot and consume themselves in little time.

23

'Were I hard-favour'd, foul, or wrinkled-old,
Ill-nurtur'd, crooked, churlish, harsh in voice,
O'erworn, despised, rheumatic and cold,
Thick-sighted, barren, lean, and lacking juice,
　Then mightest thou pause, for then I were not for thee;
　But having no defects, why does abhor me?

24

'Thou canst not see one wrinkle in my brow;
Mine eyes are grey, and bright, and quick in turning: 140
My beauty as the spring doth yearly grow,
My flesh is soft and plump, my marrow burning,
　My smooth moist hand, were it with thy hand felt,
　Would in thy palm dissolve, or seem to melt.

25

'Bid me discourse, I will enchant thine ear,
Or like a fairy trip upon the green,
Or like a nymph, with long dishevell'd hair,
Dance on the sands, and yet no footing seen.
   Love is a spirit all compact of fire,
   Not gross to sink, but light, and will aspire.   150

26

'Witness this primrose bank whereon I lie;
These forceless flowers like sturdy trees support me:
Two strengthless doves will draw me through the sky,
From morn till night, even where I list to sport me.
   Is love so light, sweet boy, and may it be
   That thou should think it heavy unto thee?

27

'Is thine own heart to thine own face affected?
Can thy right hand seize love upon thy left?
Then woo thyself, be of thyself rejected:
Steal thine own freedom, and complain on theft.   160
   Narcissus so himself himself forsook,
   And died to kiss his shadow in the brook.

28

'Torches are made to light, jewels to wear,
Dainties to taste, fresh beauty for the use,
Herbs for their smell, and sappy plants to bear.
Things growing to themselves are growth's abuse,
   Seeds spring from seeds, and beauty breedeth beauty;
   Thou wast begot; to get it is thy duty.

29

'Upon the earth's increase why shouldst thou feed,
Unless the earth with thy increase be fed?   170
By law of Nature thou art bound to breed,
That thine may live when thou thyself art dead:
   And so in spite of death thou dost survive,
   In that thy likeness still is left alive.'

30

By this, the love-sick queen began to sweat,
For where they lay the shadow had forsook them,
And Titan, tired in the midday heat,
With burning eye did hotly over-look them,
   Wishing Adonis had his team to guide,
   So he were like him, and by Venus' side.   180

31

And now Adonis, with a lazy sprite,
And with a heavy, dark disliking eye,
His louring brows o'erwhelming his fair sight,
Like misty vapours when they blot the sky,
   Souring his cheeks, cries, 'Fie, no more of love!
   The sun doth burn my face; I must remove.'

32

'Ay, me (quoth Venus) young, and so unkind!
What bare excuses mak'st thou to be gone!
I'll sigh celestial breath, whose gentle wind
Shall cool the heat of this descending sun: 190
   I'll make a shadow for thee of my hairs;
   If they burn too, I'll quench them with my tears.

33

'The sun that shines from heaven shines but warm,
And lo, I lie between that sun and thee:
The heat I have from thence doth little harm;
Thine eye darts forth the fire that burneth me,
   And were I not immortal, life were done
   Between this heavenly and earthly sun.

34

'Art thou obdurate, flinty, hard as steel?
Nay, more than flint, for stone at rain relenteth: 200
Art thou a woman's son and canst not feel
What 'tis to love, how want of love tormenteth?
   O, had thy mother borne so hard a mind,
   She had not brought forth thee, but died unkind.

35

'What am I that thou shouldst contemn me this?
Or what great danger dwells upon my suit?
What were thy lips the worse for one poor kiss?
Speak, fair, but speak fair words, or else be mute:
   Give me one kiss, I'll give it thee again,
   And one for int'rest, if thou wilt have twain.   210

36

'Fie, lifeless picture, cold and senseless stone,
Well-painted idol, image dull and dead,
Statue contenting but the eye alone,
Thing like a man, but of no woman bred!
   Thou art no man, though of a man's complexion,
   For men will kiss even by their own direction.'

37

This said, impatience chokes her pleading tongue,
And swelling passion doth provoke a pause;
Red cheeks and fiery eyes blaze forth her wrong:
Being judge in love, she cannot right her cause.   220
   And now she weeps, and now she fain would speak,
   And now her sobs do her intendments break.

38

Sometimes she shakes her head, and then his hand,
Now gazeth she on him, now on the ground;
Sometime her arms enfold him like a band;
She would, he will not in her arms be bound:
   And when from thence he struggles to be gone,
   She locks her lily fingers one in one.

39

'Fondling,' she saith, 'since I have hemm'd thee here
Within the circuit of this ivory pale,   230
I'll be a park, and thou shalt be my deer:
Feed where thou wilt, on mountain or in dale;
   Graze on my lips, and if those hills be dry,
   Stray lower, where the pleasant fountains lie.

40

'Within this limit is relief enough,
Sweet bottom-grass, and high delightful plain,
Round rising hillocks, brakes obscure and rough,
To shelter thee from tempest and from rain:
    Then be my deer, since I am such a park;
    No dog shall rouse thee, though a thousand bark.'   240

41

At this Adonis smiles as in disdain,
That in each cheek appears a pretty dimple;
Love made those hollows, if himself were slain,
He might be buried in a tomb so simple;
    Foreknowing well, if there he came to lie,
    Why, there Love liv'd, and there he could not die.

42

These lovely caves, these round enchanting pits,
Open'd their mouths to swallow Venus' liking:
Being mad before, how doth she now for wits?
Struck dead at first, what needs a second striking?   250
    Poor Queen of Love, in thine own law forlorn,
    To love a cheek that smiles at thee in scorn!

43

Now which way shall she turn? what shall she say?
Her words are done, her woes the more increasing;
The time is spent, her object will away,
And from her twining arms doth urge releasing:
    'Pity,' she cries, 'some favour, some remorse!'
    Away he springs, and hasteth to his horse.

44

But lo, from forth a copse that neighbours by,
A breeding jennet, lusty, young and proud,   260
Adonis' trampling courser doth espy
And forth she rushes, snorts, and neighs aloud.
    The strong-neck'd steed, being tied unto a tree,
    Breaketh his rein and to her straight goes he.

45

Imperiously he leaps, he neighs, he bounds,
And now his woven girths he breaks asunder;
The bearing earth with his hard hoof he wounds,
Whose hollow womb resounds like heaven's thunder,
    The iron bit he crusheth 'tween his teeth,
    Controlling what he was controlled with.   270

46

His ears up-prick'd; his braided hanging mane
Upon his compass'd crest now stand on end;
His nostrils drink the air, and forth again,
As from a furnace, vapours doth he send:
    His eye, which scornfully glisters like fire,
    Shows his hot courage and his high desire.

47

Sometime he trots, as if he told the steps,
With gentle majesty and modest pride,
Anon he rears upright, curvets, and leaps,
As who should say, 'Lo, thus my strength is tried.   280
    And this I do to captivate the eye
    Of the fair breeder that is standing by.'

48

What recketh he his rider's angry stir,
His flattering 'holla' or his 'stand, I say'?
What cares he now for curb or pricking spur,
For rich caparisons* or trappings gay?
    He sees his love, and nothing else he sees,
    For nothing else with his proud sight agrees.

49

Look when a painter would surpass the life
In limning out a well-proportion'd steed,   290
His art with Nature's workmanship at strife,
As if the dead the living should exceed:
    So did this horse excel a common one
    In shape, in courage, colour, pace and bone.

50

Round-hoof'd, short-jointed, fetlocks shag and long,
Broad breast, full eye, small head, and nostril wide,
High crest, short ears, straight legs and passing strong,
Thin mane, thick tail, broad buttock, tender hide:
   Look what a horse should have he did not lack,
   Save a proud rider on so proud a back.   300

51

Sometimes he scuds far off, and there he stares;
Anon he starts at stirring of a feather:
To bid the wind a base he now prepares,
And whe'r he run, or fly, they know not whether:
   For through his mane and tail the high wind sings,
   Fanning the hairs, who wave like feather'd wings.

52

He looks upon his love, and neighs unto her;
She answers him as if she knew his mind;
Being proud, as females are, to see him woo her,
She puts on outward strangeness, seems unkind: 310
   Spurns at his love, and scorns the heat he feels,
   Beating his kind embracements with her heels.

53

Then like a melancholy malcontent,
He vails his tail, that like a falling plume
Cool shadow to his melting buttock lent;
He stamps, and bites the poor flies in his fume:
   His love, perceiving how he was enrag'd,
   Grew kinder, and his fury was assuag'd.

54

His testy master goeth about to take him,
When, lo, the unback'd breeder, full of fear,   320
Jealous of catching, swiftly doth forsake him,
With her the horse, and left Adonis there:
   As they were mad unto the wood they hie them,
   Outstripping crows that strive to overfly them.

55

All swoln with chafing, down Adonis sits,
Banning his boist'rous and unruly beast;
And now the happy season once more fits
That lovesick love by pleading may be blest:
　　For lovers say the heart hath treble wrong
　　When it is barr'd the aidance of the tongue.　　　　330

56

An oven that is stopp'd, or river stay'd,
Burneth more hotly, swelleth with more rage:
So of concealed sorrow may be said,
Free vent of words love's fire doth assuage;
　　But when the heart's attorney once is mute,
　　The client breaks, as desperate in his suit.

57

He sees her coming, and begins to glow,
Even as a dying coal revives with wind,
And with his bonnet hides his angry brow,
Looks on the dull earth with disturbed mind:　　　　340
　　Taking no notice that she is so nigh,
　　For all askance he holds her in his eye.

58

O, what a sight it was, wistly to view
How she came stealing to the wayward boy;
To note the fighting conflict of her hue,
How white and red each other did destroy:
　　But now her cheek was pale, and by and by,
　　It flash'd forth fire, as lightning from the sky.

59

Now was she just before him as he sat,
And like a lowly lover down she kneels;
With one fair hand she heaveth up his hat,　　　　350
Her other tender hand his fair cheek feels:
　　His tenderer cheek receives her soft hand's print
　　As apt as new-fall'n snow takes any dint.

60

O, what a war of looks was then between them,
Her eyes petitioners to his eyes suing!
His eyes saw her eyes as they had not seen them,
Her eyes woo'd still, his eyes disdain'd the wooing:
   And all this dumb play had his acts made plain
   With tears which Chorus-like her eyes did rain.   360

61

Full gently now she takes him by the hand,
A lily prison'd in a gaol of snow,
Or ivory in an alabaster band;
So white a friend engirts so white a foe:
   This beauteous combat, wilful and unwilling,
   Show'd like two silver doves that sit a-billing.

62

Once more the engine of her thoughts began:
'O fairest mover on this mortal round,
Would thou wert as I am, and I a man,
My heart all whole as thine, thy heart my wound;   370
   For one sweet look thy help I would assure thee,
   Though nothing but my body's bane would cure thee.'

63

'Give me my hand (saith he), why dost thou feel it?'
'Give me my heart (saith she), and thou shalt have it.
O, give it me lest thy hard heart do steel it,
And being steel'd, soft sighs can never grave it.
   Then love's deep groans I never shall regard,
   Because Adonis' heart hath made mine hard.'

64

'For shame,' he cries, 'let go, and let me go;
My day's delight is past, my horse is gone,   380
And 'tis your fault I am bereft him so.
I pray you hence, and leave me here alone,
   For all my mind, my thought, my busy care,
   Is how to get my palfrey from the mare.'

65

Thus she replies: 'Thy palfrey, as he should,
Welcomes the warm approach of sweet desire.
Affection is a coal that must be cool'd;
Else, suffer'd, it will set the heart on fire;
    The sea hath bounds, but deep desire hath none,
    Therefore no marvel though thy horse be gone.   390

66

'How like a jade he stood tied to the tree,
Servilely master'd with a leathern rein!
But when he saw his love, his youth's fair fee,
He held such petty bondage in disdain:
    Throwing the base thong from his bending crest,
    Enfranchising his mouth, his back, his breast.

67

'Who sees his true-love in her naked bed,
Teaching the sheets a whiter hue than white,
But when his glutton eye so full hath fed,
His other agents aim at like delight?   400
    Who is so faint that dares not be so bold
    To touch the fire, the weather being cold?

68

'Let me excuse thy courser, gentle boy,
And learn of him, I heartily beseech thee,
To take advantage on presented joy;
Though I were dumb, yet his proceedings teach thee:
    O, learn to love, the lesson is but plain,
    And once made perfect, never lost again.'

69

'I know not love (quoth he) nor will not know it,
Unless it be a boar, and then I chase it.   410
'Tis much to borrow, and I will not owe it;
My love to love is love but to disgrace it,
    For I have heard it is a life in death,
    That laughs and weeps, and all but with a breath.

70

'Who wears a garment shapeless and unfinish'd?
Who plucks the bud before one leaf put forth?
If springing things be any jot diminish'd,
They wither in their prime, prove nothing worth;
    The colt that's back'd and burden'd being young
    Loseth his pride, and never waxeth strong.   420

71

'You hurt my hand with wringing; let us part,
And leave this idle theme, this bootless chat;
Remove your siege from my unyielding heart;
To love's alarms it will not ope the gate,
    Dismiss your vows, your feigned tears, your flattery,
    For where a heart is hard they make no battery.'

72

'What, canst thou talk (quoth she), hast thou a tongue?
O, wouldst thou hadst not, or I had no hearing!
Thy mermaid's voice hath done me double wrong;
I had my load before, now press'd with bearing;   430
    Melodious discord, heavenly tune harsh sounding,
    Ear's deep-sweet music, and heart's deep-sore wounding.

73

'Had I no eyes but ears, my ears would love
That inward beauty and invisible;
Or were I deaf, thy outward parts would move
Each part in me that were but sensible;
    Though neither eyes nor ears, to hear nor see,
    Yet should I be in love by touching thee.

74

'Say that the sense of feeling were bereft me,
And that I could not see, nor hear, nor touch,   440
And nothing but the very smell were left me,
Yet would my love to thee be still as much;
    For from the stillitory of thy face excelling
    Comes breath perfum'd, that breedeth love by smelling.

75

'But O, what banquet wert thou to the taste,
Being nurse and feeder of the other four!
Would they not wish the feast might ever last,
And bid suspicion double-lock the door;
　　Lest jealousy, that sour unwelcome guest,
　　Should by his stealing in disturb the feast?'　　　　450

76

Once more the ruby-colour'd portal open'd,
Which to his speech did honey passage yield,
Like a red morn that ever yet betoken'd
Wrack to the seaman, tempest to the field,
　　Sorrow to shepherds, woe unto the birds,
　　Gusts and foul flaws to herdmen and to herds.

77

This ill presage advisedly she marketh.
Even as the wind is hush'd before it raineth,
Or as the wolf doth grin before he barketh,
Or as the berry breaks before it staineth,　　　　460
　　Or like the deadly bullet of a gun,
　　His meaning struck her ere his words begun.

78

And at his look she flatly falleth down,
For looks kill love, and love by looks reviveth;
A smile recures the wounding of a frown,
But blessed bankrupt that by loss so thriveth!
　　The silly boy, believing she is dead,
　　Claps her pale cheek, till clapping makes it red.

79

And all amaz'd brake off his late intent,
For sharply he did think to reprehend her,　　　　470
Which cunning love did wittily prevent;
Fair fall the wit that can so well defend her:
　　For on the grass she lies as she were slain,
　　Till his breath breatheth life in her again.

80

He wrings her nose, he strikes her on the cheeks,
He bends her fingers, holds her pulses hard,
He chafes her lips, a thousand ways he seeks
To mend the hurt that his unkindness marr'd;
   He kisses her, and she, by her good will,
   Will never rise, so he will kiss her still.   480

81

The night of sorrow now is turn'd to day.
Her two blue windows faintly she upheaveth,
Like the fair sun when in his fresh array
He cheers the morn, and all the earth relieveth:
   And as the bright sun glorifies the sky,
   So is her face illumin'd with her eye;

82

Whose beams upon his hairless face are fix'd,
As if from thence they borrow'd all their shine;
Were never four such lamps together mix'd,
Had not his clouded with his brow's repine.   490
   But hers, which through the crystal tears gave light,
   Shone like the moon in water seen by night.

83

'O, where am I (quoth she), in earth or heaven,
Or in the ocean drench'd, or in the fire?
What hour is this, or morn or weary even?
Do I delight to die or life desire?
   But now I liv'd, and life was death's annoy.
   But now I died, and death was lively joy.

84

O, thou didst kill me; kill me once again.
Thy eyes' shrewd tutor, that hard heart of thine,   500
Hath taught them scornful tricks, and such disdain
That they have murd'red this poor heart of mine;
   And these mine eyes, true leaders to their queen,
   But for thy piteous lips no more had seen.

85

'Long may they kiss each other for this cure!
Oh, never let their crimson liveries wear,
And as they last, their verdure still endure,
To drive infection from the dangerous year!
That the star-gazers, having writ on death,
May say, the plague is banish'd by thy breath.   510

86

'Pure lips, sweet seals in my soft lips imprinted,
What bargains may I make still to be sealing?
To sell myself I can be well contented,
So thou wilt buy, and pay, and use good dealing;
Which purchase if thou make, for fear of slips,
Set thy seal manual on my wax-red lips.

87

'A thousand kisses buys my heart from me,
And pay them at thy leisure, one by one.
What is ten hundred touches unto thee?
Are they not quickly told, and quickly gone?   520
Say for non-payment that the debt should double,
Is twenty hundred kisses such a trouble?

88

'Fair queen (quoth he), if any love you owe me,
Measure my strangeness with my unripe years;
Before I know myself, seek not to know me;
No fisher but the ungrown fry forbears;
The mellow plum doth fall, the green sticks fast,
Or being early pluck'd is sour to taste.

89

'Look, the world's comforter with weary gait
His day's hot task hath ended in the west;   530
The owl (night's herald) shrieks; 'tis very late,
The sheep are gone to fold, birds to their nest,
And coal-black clouds, that shadow heaven's light,
Do summon us to part, and bid good night.

90

'Now let me say good night, and so say you;
If you will say so, you shall have a kiss.'
'Good night' (quoth she), and ere he says adieu,
The honey fee of parting tender'd is;
    Her arms do lend his neck a sweet embrace,
    Incorporate then they seem, face grows to face.   540

91

Till breathless he disjoin'd, and backward drew
The heavenly moisture, that sweet coral mouth,
Whose precious taste her thirsty lips well knew,
Whereon they surfeit, yet complain on drouth.
    He with her plenty press'd, she faint with dearth,
    Their lips together glued, fall to the earth.

92

Now quick desire hath caught the yielding prey,
And glutton-like she feeds, yet never filleth;
Her lips are conquerors, his lips obey,
Paying what ransom the insulter willeth: 550
    Whose vulture thought doth pitch the price so high,
    That she will draw his lips' rich treasure dry.

93

And having felt the sweetness of the spoil,
With blindfold fury she begins to forage;
Her face doth reek and smoke, her blood doth boil,
And careless lust stirs up a desperate courage,
    Planting oblivion, beating reason back,
    Forgetting shame's pure blush and honour's wrack.

94

Hot, faint and weary with her hard embracing,
Like a wild bird being tam'd with too much handling,   560
Or as the fleet-foot roe that's tir'd with chasing,
Or like the froward infant still'd with dandling,
    He now obeys, and now no more resisteth,
    While she takes all she can, not all she listeth.

95

What wax so frozen but dissolves with temp'ring,
And yields at last to every light impression?
Things out of hope are compass'd oft with vent'ring,
Chiefly in love, whose leave exceeds commission:
  Affection faints not like a pale-fac'd coward,
  But then woos best when most his choice is froward.   570

96

When he did frown, oh, had she then gave over,
Such nectar from his lips she had not suck'd.
Foul words and frowns must not repel a lover;
What though the rose have prickles, yet 'tis pluck'd?
  Were beauty under twenty locks kept fast,
  Yet love breaks through, and picks them all at last.

97

For pity now she can no more detain him;
The poor fool prays her that he may depart.
She is resolv'd no longer to restrain him;
Bids him farewell, and look well to her heart,
  The which by Cupid's bow she doth protest
  He carries thence incaged in his breast.   580

98

'Sweet boy,' she says, 'this night I'll waste in sorrow,
For my sick heart commands mine eyes to watch.
Tell me, Love's master, shall we meet tomorrow?
Say, shall we? shall we? wilt thou make the match?'
  He tells her no; tomorrow he intends
  To hunt the boar with certain of his friends.

99

'The boar' (quoth she): whereat a sudden pale,
Like lawn being spread upon the blushing rose,   590
Usurps her cheek; she trembles at his tale,
And on his neck her yoking arms she throws.
  She sinketh down, still hanging by his neck,
  He on her belly falls, she on her back.

100

Now is she in the very lists of love,
Her champion mounted for the hot encounter,
All is imaginary she doth prove;
He will not manage her, although he mount her;
   That worse than Tantalus' is her annoy,
   To clip Elysium and to lack her joy.   600

101

Even as poor birds deceiv'd with painted grapes
Do surfeit by the eye, and pine the maw:
Even so she languished in her mishaps
As those poor birds that helpless berries saw;
   The warm effects which she in him finds missing
   She seeks to kindle with continual kissing.

102

But all in vain, good queen, it will not be,
She hath assay'd as much as may be prov'd;
Her pleading hath deserv'd a greater fee;
She's Love; she loves, and yet she is not lov'd: 610
   'Fie, fie,' he says, 'you crush me, let me go;
   You have no reason to withhold me so.'

103

'Thou hadst been gone (quoth she), sweet boy, ere this,
But that thou told'st me thou wouldst hunt the boar.
O, be advis'd, thou know'st not what it is
With javelin's point a churlish swine to gore,
   Whose tushes never sheath'd he whetteth, still,
   Like to a mortal butcher bent to kill.

104

'On his bow-back he hath a battle set
Of bristly pikes that ever threat his foes;   620
His eyes like glow-worms shine when he doth fret;
His snout digs sepulchres where'er he goes;
   Being mov'd he strikes what'er is in his way,
   And whom he strikes his crooked tushes slay.

105

'His brawny sides, with hairy bristles arm'd,
Are better proof than thy spear's point can enter;
His short thick neck cannot be easily harm'd;
Being ireful, on the lion he will venter;
   The thorny brambles and embracing bushes,
   As fearful of him, part, through whom he rushes.   630

106

'Alas, he nought esteems that face of thine,
To which Love's eyes pays tributary gazes;
Nor thy soft hands, sweet lips and crystal eyne,
Whose full perfection all the world amazes;
   But having thee at vantage (wondrous dread!)
   Would root these beauties as he roots the mead.

107

'O, let him keep his loathsome cabin still;
Beauty hath nought to do with such foul fiends;
Come not within his danger by thy will;
They that thrive well take counsel of their friends: 640
   When thou didst name the boar, not to dissemble,
   I fear'd thy fortune, and my joints did tremble.

108

'Didst thou not mark my face, was it not white?
Saw'st thou not signs of fear lurk in mine eye?
Grew I not faint? and fell I not downright?
Within my bosom, whereon thou dost lie,
   My boding heart pants, beats and takes no rest,
   But like an earthquake shakes thee on my breast.

109

'For where Love reigns, disturbing Jealousy
Doth call himself Affection's sentinel;   650
Gives false alarms, suggesteth mutiny,
And in a peaceful hour doth cry, "Kill, kill!";
   Distemp'ring gentle Love in his desire,
   As air and water do abate the fire.

110

'This sour informer, this bate-breeding spy,
This canker that eats up Love's tender spring,
This carry-tale, dissentious Jealousy,
That sometime true news, sometime false doth bring,
   Knocks at my heart, and whispers in mine ear
   That if I love thee, I thy death should fear;   660

111

'And more than so, presenteth to mine eye
The picture of an angry chafing boar,
Under whose sharp fangs on his back doth lie
An image like thyself, all stain'd with gore;
   Whose blood upon the fresh flowers being shed
   Doth make them droop with grief and hang the head.

112

'What should I do, seeing thee so indeed,
That tremble at th' imagination?
The thought of it doth make my faint heart bleed,
And fear doth teach it divination;   670
   I prophesy thy death, my living sorrow,
   If thou encounter with the boar tomorrow.

113

'But if thou needs wilt hunt, be rul'd by me;
Uncouple at the timorous flying hare,
Or at the fox which lives by subtlety,
Or at the roe which no encounter dare:
   Pursue these fearful creatures o'er the downs,
   And on thy well-breath'd horse keep with thy hounds.

114

'And when thou hast on foot the purblind hare,
Mark the poor wretch, to overshoot his troubles,   680
How he outruns the wind, and with what care
He cranks and crosses with a thousand doubles;
   The many musits through the which he goes
   Are like a labyrinth to amaze his foes.

115

'Sometime he runs among a flock of sheep,
To make the cunning hounds mistake their smell,
And sometime where earth-delving conies keep,
To stop the loud pursuers in their yell:
   And sometime sorteth with a herd of deer;
   Danger deviseth shifts, wit waits on fear.   690

116

'For there his smell with others being mingl'd,
The hot scent-snuffing hounds are driven to doubt,
Ceasing their clamorous cry till they have singl'd
With much ado the cold fault cleanly out;
   Then do they spend their mouths; Echo replies,
   As if another chase were in the skies.

117

'By this poor Wat,* far off upon a hill,
Stands on his hinder-legs with list'ning ear,
To hearken if his foes pursue him still;
Anon their loud alarums he doth hear,   700
   And now his grief may be compared well
   To one sore sick that hears the passing-bell.

118

'Then shalt thou see the dew-bedabbled wretch
Turn and return, indenting with the way;
Each envious brier his weary legs do scratch,
Each shadow makes him stop, each murmur stay;
   For misery is trodden on by many,
   And being low, never reliev'd by any.

119

'Lie quietly, and hear a little more;
Nay, do not struggle, for thou shalt not rise.   710
To make thee hate the hunting of the boar,
Unlike myself thou hear'st me moralize,
   Applying this to that, and so to so;
   For love can comment upon every woe.

120

'Where did I leave?' 'No matter where (quoth he);
Leave me, and then the story aptly ends,
The night is spent.' 'Why, what of that?' (quoth she).
'I am (quoth he) expected of my friends;
   And now 'tis dark, and going I shall fall.'
   'In night (quoth she) desire sees best of all.'   720

121

'But if thou fall, O then imagine this,
The earth, in love with thee, thy footing trips,
And all is but to rob thee of a kiss.
Rich preys make true men thieves: so do thy lips
   Make modest Dian cloudy and forlorn,
   Lest she should steal a kiss and die forsworn.

122

'Now of this dark night I perceive the reason;
Cynthia for shame obscures her silver shine,
Till forging Nature be condemn'd of treason
For stealing moulds from heaven that were divine;   730
   Wherein she fram'd thee, in high heaven's despite,
   To shame the sun by day, and her by night.

123

'And therefore hath she brib'd the Destinies
To cross the curious workmanship of Nature,
To mingle beauty with infirmities,
And pure perfection with impure defeature,
   Making it subject to the tyranny
   Of mad mischances and much misery;

124

'As burning fevers, agues pale and faint,
Life-poisoning pestilence and frenzies wood,   740
The marrow-eating sickness whose attaint
Disorder breeds by heating of the blood,
   Surfeits, imposthumes, grief and damn'd despair,
   Swear Nature's death for framing thee so fair.

125

'And not the least of all these maladies
But in one minute's fight brings beauty under;
Both favour, savour, hue and qualities,
Whereat th' impartial gazer late did wonder,
    Are on the sudden wasted, thaw'd and done,
    As mountain snows melts with the midday sun.   750

126

'Therefore, despite of fruitless chastity,
Love-lacking vestals and self-loving nuns
That on the earth would breed a scarcity,
And barren dearth of daughters and of sons,
    Be prodigal; the lamp that burns by night
    Dries up his oil, to lend the world his light.

127

'What is thy body but a swallowing grave,
Seeming to bury that posterity
Which by the rights of time thou needs must have,
If thou destroy them not in dark obscurity?   760
    If so, the world will hold thee in disdain,
    Sith in thy pride so fair a hope is slain.

128

'So in thyself, thyself art made away;
A mischief worse than civil home-bred strife,
Or theirs whose desperate hands themselves do slay,
Or butcher sire that reaves his son of life:
    Foul cank'ring rust the hidden treasure frets,
    But gold that's put to use more gold begets.'

129

'Nay then (quoth Adonis) you will fall again
Into your idle over-handled theme;   770
The kiss I gave you is bestow'd in vain,
And all in vain you strive against the stream;
    For by this black-fac'd night, desire's foul nurse,
    Your treatise makes me like you worse and worse.

130

'If love have lent you twenty thousand tongues,
And every tongue more moving than your own,
Bewitching like the wanton mermaid's songs,
Yet from mine ear the tempting tune is blown;
  For know my heart stands armed in mine ear,
  And will not let a false sound enter there;   780

131

'Lest the deceiving harmony should run
Into the quiet closure of my breast;
And then my little heart were quite undone,
In his bedchamber to be barr'd of rest.
  No, lady, no, my heart longs not to groan,
  But soundly sleeps, while now it sleeps alone.

132

'What have you urg'd that I cannot reprove?
The path is smooth that leadeth on to danger;
I hate not love, but your device in love,
That lends embracements unto every stranger.   790
  You do it for increase! O, strange excuse
  When reason is the bawd to lust's abuse!

133

'Call it not love, for Love to heaven is fled
Since sweating Lust on earth usurp'd his name;
Under whose simple semblance he hath fed
Upon fresh Beauty, blotting it with blame;
  Which the hot tyrant stains and soon bereaves,
  As caterpillars do the tender leaves.

134

'Love comforteth like sunshine after rain,
But Lust's effect is tempest after sun;   800
Love's gentle spring doth always fresh remain,
Lust's winter comes ere summer half be done:
  Love surfeits not, Lust like a glutton dies:
  Love is all truth, Lust full of forged lies.

135

'More I could tell, but more I dare not say;
The text is old, the orator too green.
Therefore in sadness now I will away;
My face is full of shame, my heart of teen;
    Mine ears that to your wanton talk attended
    Do burn themselves for having so offended.'   810

136

With this he breaketh from the sweet embrace
Of those fair arms which bound him to her breast,
And homeward through the dark lawnd runs apace;
Leaves Love upon her back, deeply distress'd.
    Look how a bright star shooteth from the sky,
    So glides he in the night from Venus' eye;

137

Which after him she darts, as one on shore
Gazing upon a late-embarked friend,
Till the wild waves will have seen him no more,
Whose ridges with the meeting clouds contend: 820
    So did the merciless and pitchy night
    Fold in the object that did feed her sight.

138

Whereat amaz'd as one that unaware
Hath dropp'd a precious jewel in the flood,
Or 'stonish'd, as night-wand'rers often are,
Their light blown out in some mistrustful wood;
    Even so confounded in the dark she lay,
    Having lost the fair discovery of her way.

139

And now she beats her heart, whereat it groans,
That all the neighbour caves, as seeming troubled,   830
Make verbal repetition of her moans;
Passion on passion deeply is redoubled;
    'Ay me,' she cries, and twenty times, 'woe, woe!'
    And twenty echoes twenty times cry so.

140

She, marking them, begins a wailing note,
And sings extemporally a woeful ditty:
How love makes young men thrall, and old men dote,
How love is wise in folly, foolish witty;
　　Her heavy anthem still concludes in woe,
　　And still the choir of echoes answer so.   840

141

Her song was tedious and outwore the night,
For lover's hours are long, though seeming short;
If pleas'd themselves, others, they think, delight
In such-like circumstances, with such-like sport:
　　Their copious stories, oftentimes begun,
　　End without audience and are never done.

142

For who hath she to spend the night withal,
But idle sounds resembling parasites;
Like shrill-tongued tapsters answering every call,
Soothing the humour of fantastic wits?   850
　　She says "Tis so'; they answer all "Tis so';
　　And would say after her, if she said 'no'.

143

Lo, here the gentle lark, weary of rest,
From his moist cabinet mounts up on high
And wakes the morning, from whose silver breast
The sun ariseth in his majesty,
　　Who doth the world so gloriously behold
　　That cedar-tops and hills seem burnish'd gold.

144

Venus salutes him with this fair good-morrow:
'O, thou clear god, and patron of all light,   860
From whom each lamp and shining star doth borrow
The beauteous influence that makes him bright,
　　There lives a son that suck'd an earthly mother
　　May lend thee light, as thou dost lend to other.'

145

This said, she hasteth to a myrtle grove,
Musing the morning is so much o'erworn,
And yet she hears no tidings of her love;
She hearkens for his hounds and for his horn.
    Anon she hears them chant it lustily,
    And all in haste she coasteth to the cry.   870

146

And as she runs, the bushes in the way
Some catch her by the neck, some kiss her face,
Some twin'd about her thigh to make her stay;
She wildly breaketh from their strict embrace,
    Like a milch doe, whose swelling dugs do ache,
    Hasting to feed her fawn hid in some brake.

147

By this she hears the hounds are at a bay;
Whereat she starts, like one that spies an adder
Wreath'd up in fatal folds just in his way,
The fear whereof doth make him shake and shudder;   880
    Even so the timorous yelping of the hounds
    Appals her senses and her spirit confounds.

148

For now she knows it is no gentle chase,
But the blunt boar, rough bear, or lion proud,
Because the cry remaineth in one place,
Where fearfully the dogs exclaim aloud;
    Finding their enemy to be so curst,
    They all strain court'sy who shall cope him first.

149

This dismal cry rings sadly in her ear,
Through which it enters to surprise her heart;   890
Who, overcome by doubt and bloodless fear,
With cold-pale weakness numbs each feeling part;
    Like soldiers when their captain once doth yield,
    They basely fly and dare not stay the field.

150

Thus stands she in a trembling ecstasy;
Till, cheering up her senses all dismay'd,
She tells them 'tis a causeless fantasy,
And childish error, that they are afraid;
  Bids them leave quaking, bids them fear no more.
  And with that word she spied the hunted boar,   900

151

Whose frothy mouth, bepainted all with red,
Like milk and blood being mingled both together,
A second fear through all her sinews spread,
Which madly hurries her, she knows not whither;
  This way she runs, and now she will no further,
  But back retires, to rate the boar for murder.

152

A thousand spleens bear her a thousand ways;
She treads the path that she untreads again;
Her more than haste is mated with delays,
Like the proceedings of a drunken brain,   910
  Full of respects, yet not at all respecting,
  In hand with all things, nought at all effecting.

153

Here kennell'd in a brake she finds a hound,
And asks the weary caitiff for his master;
And there another licking of his wound,
'Gainst venom'd sores the only sovereign plaster;
  And here she meets another, sadly scowling,
  To whom she speaks, and he replies with howling.

154

When he hath ceas'd his ill-resounding noise,
Another flap-mouth'd mourner, black and grim,   920
Against the welkin volleys out his voice;
Another, and another, answer him,
  Clapping their proud tails to the ground below,
  Shaking their scratch'd ears, bleeding as they go.

155

Look how the world's poor people are amaz'd
At apparitions, signs and prodigies,
Whereon with fearful eyes they long have gaz'd,
Infusing them with dreadful prophecies;
　　So she at these sad signs draws up her breath,
　　And sighing it again, exclaims on Death.   930

156

'Hard-favoured tyrant, ugly, meagre, lean,
Hateful divorce of love, (thus chides she Death)
Grim-grinning ghost, earth's worm, what dost thou mean
To stifle beauty, and to steal his breath
　　Who when he liv'd, his breath and beauty set
　　Gloss on the rose, smell to the violet?

157

'If he be dead – O no, it cannot be,
Seeing his beauty, thou shouldst strike at it –
O yes, it may; thou hast no eyes to see,
But hatefully at random dost thou hit;   940
　　Thy mark is feeble age, but thy false dart
　　Mistakes that aim, and cleaves an infant's heart.

158

'Hadst thou but bid beware, then he had spoke,
And hearing him, thy power had lost his power.
The Destinies will curse thee for this stroke;
They bid thee crop a weed, thou pluck'st a flower;
　　Love's golden arrow at him should have fled,
　　And not Death's ebon dart, to strike him dead.

159

'Dost thou drink tears, that thou provok'st such weeping;
What may a heavy groan advantage thee?   950
Why hast thou cast into eternal sleeping
Those eyes that taught all other eyes to see?
　　Now Nature cares not for thy mortal vigour,
　　Since her best work is ruin'd with thy rigour.'

160

Here overcome as one full of despair,
She vail'd her eye-lids, who like sluices stopp'd
The crystal tide that from her two cheeks fair
In the sweet channel of her bosom dropp'd:
  But through the flood-gates breaks the silver rain,
  And with his strong course opens them again.   960

161

O, how her eyes and tears did lend and borrow!
Her eye seen in the tears, tears in her eye;
Both crystals, where they view'd each other's sorrow,
Sorrow that friendly sighs sought still to dry;
  But like a stormy day, now wind, now rain,
  Sighs dry her cheeks, tears make them wet again.

162

Variable passions throng her constant woe,
As striving who should best become her grief;
All entertain'd, each passion labours so
That every present sorrow seemeth chief,   970
  But none is best. Then join they all together,
  Like many clouds consulting for foul weather.

163

By this, far off she hears some huntsman holla;
A nurse's song ne'er pleased her babe so well.
The dire imagination she did follow
This sound of hope doth labour to expel;
  For now reviving joy bids her rejoice,
  And flatters her, it is Adonis' voice.

164

Whereat her tears began to turn their tide,
Being prison'd in her eye like pearls in glass.   980
Yet sometimes falls an orient drop beside,
Which her cheek melts, as scorning it should pass
  To wash the foul face of the sluttish ground,
  Who is but drunken when she seemeth drown'd.

165

O, hard-believing love, how strange it seems
Not to believe, and yet too credulous!
Thy weal and woe are both of them extremes;
Despair and hope makes thee ridiculous:
   The one doth flatter thee in thoughts unlikely,
   In likely thoughts the other kills thee quickly.   990

166

Now she unweaves the web that she hath wrought;
Adonis lives, and Death is not to blame:
It was not she that call'd him all to nought;
Now she adds honours to his hateful name.
   She clepes him king of graves, and grave for kings,
   Imperious supreme of all mortal things.

167

'No, no,' quoth she, 'sweet Death, I did but jest;
Yet pardon me, I felt a kind of fear
Whenas I met the boar, that bloody beast
Which knows no pity but is still severe.   1000
   Then, gentle shadow, (truth I must confess)
   I rail'd on thee, fearing my love's decease.

168

"Tis not my fault; the boar provok'd my tongue;
Be wreak'd on him (invisible commander);
'Tis he, foul creature, that hath done thee wrong;
I did but act, he's author of thy slander.
   Grief hath two tongues, and never woman yet
   Could rule them both without ten women's wit.'

169

Thus, hoping that Adonis is alive,
Her rash suspect she doth extenuate;   1010
And that his beauty may the better thrive,
With Death she humbly doth insinuate;
   Tells him of trophies, statues, tombs, and stories
   His victories, his triumphs and his glories.

170

'O Jove,' quoth she, 'how much a fool was I
To be of such a weak and silly mind
To wail his death who lives, and must not die
Till mutual overthrow of mortal kind!
  For he being dead, with him is Beauty slain,
  And Beauty dead, black Chaos comes again!   1020

171

'Fie, fie, fond Love, thou art as full of fear
As one with treasure laden, hemm'd with thieves;
Trifles unwitnessed with eye or ear
Thy coward heart with false bethinking grieves.'
  Even at this word she hears a merry horn,
  Whereat she leaps that was but late forlorn.

172

As falcons to the lure, away she flies;
The grass stoops not, she treads on it so light;
And in her haste unfortunately spies
The foul boar's conquest on her fair delight;   1030
  Which seen, her eyes as murd'red with the view,
  Like stars asham'd of day, themselves withdrew;

173

Or as the snail, whose tender horns being hit,
Shrinks backward in his shelly cave with pain,
And, there all smother'd up, in shade doth sit,
Long after fearing to creep forth again:
  So at his bloody view her eyes are fled
  Into the deep-dark cabins of her head;

174

Where they resign their office and their light
To the disposing of her troubled brain,   1040
Who bids them still consort with ugly night,
And never wound the heart with looks again;
  Who, like a king perplexed in his throne,
  By their suggestion gives a deadly groan,

175

Whereat each tributary subject quakes;
As when the wind, imprison'd in the ground,
Struggling for passage, earth's foundation shakes,
Which with cold terror doth men's minds confound.
  This mutiny each part doth so surprise,
  That from their dark beds once more leap her eyes;   1050

176

And being open'd, threw unwilling light
Upon the wide wound that the boar had trench'd
In his soft flank, whose wonted lily white
With purple tears that his wound wept was drench'd.
  No flower was nigh, no grass, herb, leaf or weed,
  But stole his blood and seem'd with him to bleed.

177

This solemn sympathy poor Venus noteth;
Over one shoulder doth she hang her head,
Dumbly she passions, franticly she doteth;
She thinks he could not die, he is not dead.   1060
  Her voice is stopp'd, her joints forget to bow;
  Her eyes are mad that they have wept till now.

178

Upon his hurts she looks so steadfastly
That her sight dazzling makes the wound seem three,
And then she reprehends her mangling eye
That makes more gashes where no breach should be:
  His face seems twain, each several limb is doubled;
  For oft the eye mistakes, the brain being troubled.

179

'My tongue cannot express my grief for one,
And yet (quoth she) behold two Adons dead!   1070
My sighs are blown away, my salt tears gone,
Mine eyes are turn'd to fire, my heart to lead;
  Heavy heart's lead, melt at mine eyes' red fire!
  So shall I die by drops of hot desire.

180

'Alas, poor world, what treasure hast thou lost!
What face remains alive that's worth the viewing?
Whose tongue is music now? what canst thou boast
Of things long since, or anything ensuing?
   The flowers are sweet, their colours fresh, and trim;
   But true sweet Beauty liv'd and died with him.   1080

181

'Bonnet nor veil henceforth no creature wear,
Nor sun nor wind will ever strive to kiss you;
Having no fair to lose, you need not fear
The sun doth scorn you, and the wind doth hiss you.
   But when Adonis liv'd, sun and sharp air
   Lurk'd like two thieves to rob him of his fair.

182

'And therefore would he put his bonnet on,
Under whose brim the gaudy sun would peep;
The wind would blow it off, and being gone,
Play with his locks. Then would Adonis weep;   1090
   And straight, in pity of his tender years,
   They both would strive who first should dry his tears.

183

'To see his face the lion walk'd along
Behind some hedge, because he would not fear him:
To recreate himself when he hath song,
The tiger would be tame and gently hear him;
   If he had spoke, the wolf would leave his prey,
   And never fright the silly lamb that day.

184

'When he beheld his shadow in the brook,
The fishes spread on it their golden gills;   1100
When he was by, the birds such pleasure took
That some would sing, some others in their bills
   Would bring him mulberries and ripe-red cherries;
   He fed them with his sight, they him with berries.

185

'But this foul, grim and urchin-snouted boar,
Whose downward eye still looketh for a grave,
Ne'er saw the beauteous livery that he wore;
Witness the entertainment that he gave.
    If he did see his face, why then I know
    He thought to kiss him, and hath kill'd him so.   1110

186

''Tis true, 'tis true, thus was Adonis slain;
He ran upon the boar with his sharp spear,
Who did not whet his teeth at him again,
But by a kiss thought to persuade him there;
    And nuzzling in his flank, the loving swine
    Sheath'd unaware the tusk in his soft groin.

187

'Had I been tooth'd like him, I must confess
With kissing him I should have kill'd him first;
But he is dead, and never did he bless
My youth with his; the more I am accurst.'   1120
    With this she falleth in the place she stood,
    And stains her face with his congealed blood.

188

She looks upon his lips, and they are pale;
She takes him by the hand, and that is cold,
She whispers in his ears a heavy tale,
As if they heard the woeful words she told;
    She lifts the coffer-lids that close his eyes,
    Where, lo, two lamps, burnt out, in darkness lies;

189

Two glasses where herself herself beheld
A thousand times, and now no more reflect;   1130
Their virtue lost wherein they late excell'd,
And every beauty robb'd of his effect.
    'Wonder of time, (quoth she), this is my spite,
    That, thou being dead, the day should yet be light.

190

'Since thou art dead, lo, here I prophesy
Sorrow on love hereafter shall attend:
It shall be waited on with jealousy,
Find sweet beginning but unsavoury end;
   Ne'er settled equally, but high or low,
   That all love's pleasure shall not match his woe.   1140

191

'It shall be fickle, false and full of fraud;
Bud, and be blasted, in a breathing while;
The bottom poison, and the top o'erstraw'd
With sweets that shall the truest sight beguile;
   The strongest body shall it make most weak,
Strike the wise dumb, and teach the fool to speak.

192

'It shall be sparing, and too full of riot,
Teaching decrepit age to tread the measures;
The staring ruffian shall it keep in quiet,
Pluck down the rich, enrich the poor with treasures;   1150
   It shall be raging-mad, and silly-mild,
   Make the young old, the old become a child.

193

'It shall suspect where is no cause of fear;
It shall not fear where it should most mistrust;
It shall be merciful and too severe,
And most deceiving when it seems most just;
   Perverse it shall be where it shows most toward,
   Put fear to valour, courage to the coward.

194

'It shall be cause of war and dire events,
And set dissension 'twixt the son and sire;   1160
Subject and servile to all discontents,
As dry combustious matter is to fire,
   Sith in his prime Death doth my love destroy,
   They that love best their loves shall not enjoy.'

195

By this the boy that by her side lay kill'd
Was melted like a vapour from her sight,
And in his blood that on the ground lay spill'd
A purple flower sprung up, chequer'd with white,
   Resembling well his pale cheeks, and the blood
   Which in round drops upon their whiteness stood.   1170

196

She bows her head the new-sprung flower to smell,
Comparing it to her Adonis' breath,
And says within her bosom it shall dwell,
Since he himself is reft from her by death;
   She crops the stalk, and in the breach appears
   Green-dropping sap, which she compares to tears.

197

'Poor flower (quoth she), this was thy father's guise —
Sweet issue of a more sweet-smelling sire —
For every little grief to wet his eyes.
To grow unto himself was his desire;   1180
   And so 'tis thine; but know, it is as good
   To wither in my breast as in his blood.

198

'Here was thy father's bed, here in my breast;
Thou art the next of blood, and 'tis thy right.
Lo, in this hollow cradle take thy rest;
My throbbing heart shall rock thee day and night;
   There shall not be one minute in an hour
   Wherein I will not kiss my sweet love's flower.'

199

Thus weary of the world, away she hies,
And yokes her silver doves, by whose swift aid   1190
Their mistress, mounted, through the empty skies
In her light chariot quickly is convey'd,
   Holding their course to Paphos, where their queen
   Means to immure herself and not be seen.

Christopher Marlowe

Hero and Leander

(1598)

First Sestiad

On Hellespont* guilty of true love's blood,
In view, and opposite, two cities stood,
Sea borderers, disjoin'd by Neptune's might;
The one Abydos, the other Sestos hight.
At Sestos, Hero dwelt; Hero the fair,
Whom young Apollo courted for her hair,
And offer'd as a dower his burning throne,
Where she should sit for men to gaze upon.
The outside of her garments were of lawn,
The lining purple silk, with gilt stars drawn;   10
Her wide sleeves green, and border'd with a grove,
Where Venus in her naked glory strove
To please the careless and disdainful eyes
Of proud Adonis, that before her lies;
Her kirtle blue, whereon was many a stain,
Made with the blood of wretched lovers slain.
Upon her head she ware a myrtle wreath,
From whence her veil reach'd to the ground beneath.
Her veil was artificial flowers and leaves,
Whose workmanship both man and beast deceives.   20
Many would praise the sweet smell as she pass'd,
When 'twas the odour which her breath forth cast;
And there for honey bees have sought in vain,
And, beat from thence, have lighted there again.
About her neck hung chains of pebble-stone,
Which, lighten'd by her neck, like diamonds shone.
She ware no gloves, for neither sun nor wind
Would burn or parch her hands, but to her mind,
Or warm or cool them, for they took delight

To play upon those hands, they were so white,   30
Buskins of shells all silver'd used she,
And branch'd with blushing coral to the knee,
Where sparrows perch'd, of hollow pearl and gold,
Such as the world would wonder to behold:
Those with sweet water oft her handmaid fills,
Which, as she went, would chirrup through the hills.
Some say, for her the fairest Cupid pin'd,
And, looking in her face, was strooken blind.
But this is true, so like was one the other,
As he imagin'd Hero was his mother;   40
And oftentimes into her bosom flew,
About her naked neck his bare arms flew,
And laid his childish head upon her breast,
And with still panting rock'd, there took his rest.
So lovely fair was Hero, Venus' nun,
As Nature wept, thinking she was undone,
Because she took more from her than she left,
And of such wondrous beauty her bereft;
Therefore, in sign her treasure suffer'd wrack,
Since Hero's time hath half the world been black.   50
Amorous Leander, beautiful and young,
(Whose tragedy divine Musaeus sung)
Dwelt at Abydos; since him dwelt there none
For whom succeeding times make greater moan.
His dangling tresses that were never shorn,
Had they been cut and unto Colchos borne,
Would have allur'd the venturous youth of Greece
To hazard more than for the golden fleece.
Fair Cynthia wish'd his arms might be her sphere;
Grief makes her pale, because she moves not there.   60
His body was as straight as Circe's wand;
Jove might have sipp'd out nectar from his hand.
Even as delicious meat is to the taste,
So was his neck in touching, and surpass'd
The white of Pelops' shoulder. I could tell ye
How smooth his breast was, and how white his belly,
And whose immortal fingers did imprint
That heavenly path, with many a curious dint,
That runs along his back; but my rude pen
Can hardly blazon forth the loves of men,   70

Much less of powerful gods; let it suffice
That my slack muse sings of Leander's eyes,
Those orient cheeks and lips, exceeding his
That leapt into the water for a kiss*
Of his own shadow, and despising many,
Died ere he could enjoy the love of any.
Had wild Hippolytus Leander seen,
Enamour'd of his beauty had he been;
His presence made the rudest peasant melt,
That in the vast uplandish country dwelt;   80
The barbarous Thracian soldier, mov'd with nought,
Was mov'd with him, and for his favour sought.
Some swore he was a maid in man's attire,
For in his looks were all that men desire,
A pleasant smiling cheek, a speaking eye,
A brow for love to banquet royally;
And such as knew he was a man, would say,
'Leander, thou art made for amorous play;
Why art thou not in love, and lov'd of all?
Though thou be fair, yet be not thine own thrall.'   90
   The men of wealthy Sestos, every year,
For his sake whom their goddess held so dear,
Rose-cheek'd Adonis, kept a solemn feast.
Thither resorted many a wandering guest
To meet their loves; such as had none at all,
Came lovers home from this great festival.
For every street, like to a firmament,
Glister'd with breathing stars, who, where they went,
Frighted the melancholy earth, which deem'd
Eternal heaven to burn, for so it seem'd   100
As if another Phaeton had got
The guidance of the sun's rich chariot.
But, far above the loveliest, Hero shin'd,
And stole away th' enchanted gazer's mind;
For like sea-nymphs' inveigling harmony,*
So was her beauty to the standers-by.
Nor that night-wand'ring pale and wat'ry star
(When yawning dragons draw her thirling car
From Latmus' mount up to the gloomy sky,
Where, crown'd with blazing light and majesty,   110
She proudly sits) more over-rules the flood

Than she the hearts of those that near her stood.
Even as, when gaudy nymphs pursue the chase,
Wretched Ixion's shaggy-footed race,
Incens'd with savage heat, gallop amain
From steep pine-bearing mountains to the plain;
So ran the people forth to gaze upon her,
And all that view'd her were enamour'd on her.
And as in fury of a dreadful fight,
Their fellows being slain or put to flight,   120
Poor soldiers stand with fear of death dead strooken,
So at her presence all, surpris'd and tooken,
Await the sentence of her scornful eyes;
He whom she favours lives, the other dies.
There might you see one sigh, another rage,
And some, their violent passions to assuage,
Compile sharp satires; but alas! too late,
For faithful love will never turn to hate.
And many, seeing great princes were denied,
Pin'd as they went, and thinking on her, died.   130
On this feast day, oh, cursed day and hour!
Went Hero thorough Sestos, from her tower
To Venus' temple, where unhappily,
As after chanc'd, they did each other spy.
So fair a church as this had Venus none;
The walls were of discolour'd jasper stone,
Wherein was Proteus carv'd, and o'erhead
A lively vine of green sea-agate spread,
Where by one hand light-headed Bacchus hung,
And with the other wine from grapes out-wrung.   140
Of crystal shining fair the pavement was;
The town of Sestos call'd it Venus' glass.
There might you see the gods in sundry shapes,
Committing heady riots, incest, rapes:
For know that underneath this radiant floor
Was Danae's statue in a brazen tower;
Jove slyly stealing from his sister's bed
To dally with Idalian Ganymede,*
And for his love Europa bellowing loud,
And tumbling with the rainbow in a cloud;   150
Blood-quaffing Mars heaving the iron net
Which limping Vulcan and his Cyclops set;

Love kindling fire to burn such towns as Troy;
Silvanus weeping for the lovely boy
That now is turn'd into a cypress tree,
Under whose shade the wood-gods love to be.
And in the midst a silver altar stood;
There Hero sacrificing turtles' blood,
Vail'd to the ground, veiling her eyelids close,
And modestly they open'd as she rose: 160
Thence flew love's arrow with the golden head,
And thus Leander was enamoured.
Stone-still he stood, and evermore he gaz'd,
Till with the fire that from his countenance blaz'd
Relenting Hero's gentle heart was strook;
Such force and virtue hath an amorous look.
   It lies not in our power to love or hate,
For will in us is over-rul'd by Fate.
When two are stripp'd, long ere the course begin
We wish that one should lose, the other win;   170
And one especially do we affect
Of two gold ingots, like in each respect.
The reason no man knows; let it suffice,
What we behold is censur'd by our eyes.
Where both deliberate, the love is slight;
Who ever lov'd, that lov'd not at first sight?
   He kneel'd, but unto her devoutly pray'd;
Chaste Hero to herself thus softly said:
'Were I the saint he worships, I would hear him;'
And as she spake these words, came somewhat near him.   180
He started up; she blush'd as one asham'd;
Wherewith Leander much more was inflam'd.
He touch'd her hand; in touching it she trembl'd;
Love deeply grounded hardly is dissembl'd.
These lovers parled by the touch of hands;
True love is mute, and oft amazed stands.
Thus while dumb signs their yielding hearts entangl'd,
The air with sparks of living fire was spangl'd,
And Night, deep drench'd in misty Acheron,
Heav'd up her head, and half the world upon   190
Breath'd darkness forth (dark night is Cupid's day).
And now begins Leander to display
Love's holy fire with words, with sighs and tears,

Which like sweet music enter'd Hero's ears;
And yet at every word she turn'd aside,
And always cut him off as he replied.
At last, like to a bold sharp sophister,
With cheerful hope thus he accosted her:
    'Fair creature, let me speak without offence;
I would my rude words had the influence   200
To lead thy thoughts as thy fair looks do mine;
Then shouldst thou be his prisoner who is thine.
Be not unkind and fair; misshapen stuff
Are of behaviour boisterous and rough.
O! shun me not, but hear me ere you go;
God knows I cannot force love, as you do.
My words shall be as spotless as my youth,
Full of simplicity and naked truth.
This sacrifice, whose sweet perfume descending
From Venus' altar to your footsteps bending,   210
Doth testify that you exceed her far
To whom you offer, and whose nun you are.
Why should you worship her? her you surpass
As much as sparkling diamonds flaring glass.
A diamond set in lead his worth retains;
A heavenly nymph, belov'd of human swains,
Receives no blemish, but oft-times more grace;
Which makes me hope, although I am but base,
Base in respect of thee, divine and pure,
Dutiful service may thy love procure;   220
And I in duty will excel all other,
As thou in beauty dost exceed Love's mother.
Nor heaven, nor thou, were made to gaze upon;
As heaven preserves all things, so save thou one.
A stately-built ship, well rigg'd and tall,
The ocean maketh more majestical:
Why vowest thou then to live in Sestos here,
Who on Love's seas more glorious would appear?
Like untun'd golden strings all women are,
Which, long time lie untouch'd, will harshly jar.   230
Vessels of brass, oft handl'd, brightly shine;
What difference betwixt the richest mine
And basest mould, but use? for both, not us'd,
Are of like worth. Then treasure is abus'd,

When misers keep it; being put to loan,
In time it will return us two for one.
Rich robes themselves and others do adorn;
Neither themselves nor others, if not worn.
Who builds a palace, and rams up the gate,
Shall see it ruinous and desolate. 240
Ah, simple Hero, learn thyself to cherish;
Lone women, like to empty houses, perish.
Less sins the poor rich man that starves himself
In heaping up a mass of drossy pelf,
Than such as you; his golden earth remains,
Which after his decease some other gains;
But this fair gem, sweet in the loss alone,
When you fleet hence, can be bequeath'd to none.
Or if it could, down from th' enamell'd sky
All heaven would come to claim this legacy, 250
And with intestine broils the world destroy,
And quite confound Nature's sweet harmony.
Well therefore by the gods decreed it is
We human creatures should enjoy that bliss.
One is no number; maids are nothing, then,
Without the sweet society of men.
Wilt thou live single still? One shalt thou be
Though never-singling Hymen couple thee.
Wild savages, that drink of running springs,
Think water far excels all earthly things, 260
But they that daily taste neat wine despise it.
Virginity, albeit some highly prize it,
Compar'd with marriage, had you tried them both,
Differs as much as wine and water doth.
Base bullion for the stamp's sake we allow;
Even so for men's impression do we you,
By which alone, our reverend fathers say,
Women receive perfection every way.
This idol which you term virginity
Is neither essence subject to the eye, 270
No, nor to any one exterior sense;
Nor hath it any place of residence,
Nor is 't of earth or mould celestial,
Or capable of any form at all.
Of that which hath no being do not boast;

Things that are not at all are never lost.
Men foolishly do call it virtuous;
What virtue is it, that is born with us?
Much less can honour be ascrib'd thereto;
Honour is purchas'd by the deeds we do.   280
Believe me, Hero, honour is not won
Until some honourable deed be done.
Seek you for chastity, immortal fame,
And know that some have wrong'd Diana's name?
Whose name is it, if she be false or not,
So she be fair, but some vile tongues will blot?
But you are fair, ay me! so wondrous fair,
So young, so gentle, and so debonair,
As Greece will think, if thus you live alone,
Some one or other keeps you as his own,   290
Then, Hero, hate me not, nor from me fly,
To follow swiftly-blasting infamy.
Perhaps thy sacred priesthood makes thee loth;
Tell me, to whom madest thou that heedless oath?'
    'To Venus,' answer'd she, and as she spake,
Forth from those two tralucent cisterns brake
A stream of liquid pearl, which down her face
Make milk-white paths, whereon the gods might trace
To Jove's high court. He thus replied: 'The rites
In which Love's beauteous empress most delights   300
Are banquets, Doric music, midnight revel,
Plays, masques, and all that stern age counteth evil.
Thee as a holy idiot doth she scorn,
For thou, in vowing chastity, hast sworn
To rob her name and honour, and thereby
Commit'st a sin far worse than perjury,
Even sacrilege against her deity,
Through regular and formal purity.
To expiate which sin, kiss and shake hands;
Such sacrifice as this Venus demands.'   310
    Thereat she smil'd, and did deny him so
As, put thereby, yet might he hope for mo.
Which makes him quickly reinforce his speech,
And her in humble manner thus beseech:
'Though neither gods nor men may thee deserve,
Yet for her sake whom you have vow'd to serve,

Abandon fruitless cold virginity,
The gentle queen of love's sole enemy.
Then shall you most resemble Venus' nun,
When Venus' sweet rites are perform'd and done.   320
Flint-breasted Pallas joys in single life,
But Pallas and your mistress are at strife.
Love, Hero, then, and be not tyrannous,
But heal the heart that thou has wounded thus;
Nor stain thy youthful years with avarice;
Fair fools delight to be accounted nice.
The richest corn dies, if it be not reap'd;
Beauty alone is lost, too warily kept.'
These arguments he us'd, and many more,
Wherewith she yielded, that was won before.   330
Hero's looks yielded, but her words made war;
Women are won when they begin to jar.
Thus having swallow'd Cupid's golden hook,
The more she striv'd, the deeper was she strook;
Yet, evilly feigning anger, strove she still,
And would be thought to grant against her will.
So having paus'd a while, at last she said:
'Who taught thee rhetoric to deceive a maid?
Ay me! such words as these should I abhor,
And yet I like them for the orator.'   340
    With that Leander stoop'd to have embrac'd her,
But from his spreading arms away she cast her,
And thus bespake him: 'Gentle youth, forbear
To touch the sacred garments which I wear.
Upon a rock, and underneath a hill,
Far from the town, where all is whist and still,
Save that the sea, playing on yellow sand,
Sends forth a rattling murmur to the land,
Whose sound allures the golden Morpheus
In silence of the night to visit us,   350
My turret stands; and there, God knows, I play
With Venus' swans and sparrows all the day.
A dwarfish beldame bears me company,
That hops about the chamber where I lie,
And spends the night, that might be better spent,
In vain discourse and apish merriment.
Come thither.' As she spake this, her tongue tripp'd.

For unawares 'Come thither' from her slipp'd;
And suddenly her former colour chang'd,
And here and there her eyes through anger rang'd.   360
And like a planet moving several ways
At one self instant, she, poor soul, assays,
Loving, not to love at all, and every part
Strove to resist the motions of her heart:
And hands so pure, so innocent, nay such
As might have made heaven stoop to have a touch,
Did she uphold to Venus, and again
Vow'd spotless chastity, but all in vain.
Cupid beats down her prayers with his wings;
Her vows above the empty air he flings;   370
All deep enrag'd, his sinewy bow he bent,
And shot a shaft that burning from him went;
Wherewith she strooken look'd so dolefully
As made Love sigh to see his tyranny.
And as she wept, her tears to pearl he turn'd,
And wound them on his arm, and for her mourn'd.
Then towards the palace of the Destinies,
Laden with the languishment and grief, he flies,
And to those stern nymphs humbly made request,
Both might enjoy each other, and be blest.   380
But with a ghastly dreadful countenance,
Threatening a thousand deaths at every glance,
They answer'd Love, nor would vouchsafe so much
As one poor word, their hate to him was such.
Hearken awhile, and I will tell you why:
Heaven's winged herald, Jove-born Mercury,
The self-same day that he asleep had laid
Enchanted Argus, spied a country maid,
Whose careless hair, instead of pearl t' adorn it,
Glister'd with dew, as one that seem'd to scorn it: 390
Her breath as fragrant as the morning rose,
Her mind pure, and her tongue untaught to gloze;
Yet proud she was, for lofty pride that dwells
In tower'd courts is oft in shepherds' cells,
And too too well the fair vermilion knew,
And silver tincture of her cheeks, that drew
The love of every swain. On her this god
Enamour'd was, and with his snaky rod

Did charm her nimble feet, and made her stay,
The while upon a hillock down he lay,   400
And sweetly on his pipe began to play,
And with smooth speech her fancy to assay;
Till in his twining arms he lock'd her fast,
And then he woo'd with kisses, and at last,
As shepherds do, her on the ground he laid,
And tumbling in the grass, he often stray'd
Beyond the bounds of shame, in being bold
To eye those parts which no eye should behold;
And like an insolent commanding lover,
Boasting his parentage, would needs discover   410
The way to new Elysium: but she,
Whose only dower was her chastity,
Having striven in vain, was now about to cry,
And crave the help of shepherds that were nigh.
Herewith he stay'd his fury, and began
To give her leave to rise; away she ran;
After went Mercury, who us'd such cunning
As she, to hear his tale, left off her running.
Maids are not won by brutish force and might,
But speeches full of pleasure and delight;   420
And knowing Hermes courted her, was glad
That she such loveliness and beauty had
As could provoke his liking, yet was mute,
And neither would deny nor grant his suit.
Still vow'd he love; she, wanting no excuse
To feed him with delays, as women use,
Or thirsting after immortality –
All women are ambitious naturally –
Impos'd upon her lover such a task
As he ought not perform, nor yet she ask.   430
A draught of flowing nectar she requested,
Wherewith the king of gods and men is feasted.
He, ready to accomplish what she will'd,
Stole some from Hebe (Hebe Jove's cup fill'd)
And gave it to his simple rustic love;
Which being known (as what is hid from Jove?)
He inly storm'd, and wax'd more furious
Than for the fire filch'd by Prometheus,
And thrusts him down from heaven: he wandering here,

In mournful terms, with sad and heavy cheer,   440
Complain'd to Cupid. Cupid, for his sake,
To be reveng'd on Jove did undertake;
And those on whom heaven, earth, and hell relies,
I mean the adamantine Destinies,
He wounds with love, and forc'd them equally
To dote upon deceitful Mercury.
They offer'd him the deadly fatal knife
That shears the slender threads of human life;
At his fair feather'd feet the engines laid
Which th' earth from ugly Chaos' den upway'd.   450
These he regarded not, but did entreat
That Jove, usurper of his father's seat,
Might presently be banish'd into hell,
And aged Saturn in Olympus dwell.
They granted what he crav'd, and once again
Saturn and Ops began their golden reign.
Murder, rape, war, lust, and treachery
Were with Jove clos'd in Stygian empery.
But long this blessed time continu'd not;
As soon as he his wished purpose got,   460
He, reckless of his promise, did despise
The love of th' everlasting Destinies.
They seeing it, both Love and him abhorr'd,
And Jupiter unto his place restor'd.
And but that Learning, in despite of Fate,
Will mount aloft, and enter heaven gate,
And to the seat of Jove itself advance,
Hermes had slept in hell with Ignorance;
Yet as a punishment they added this,
That he and poverty should always kiss.   470
And to this day is every scholar poor;
Gross gold from them runs headlong to the boor.
Likewise, the angry sisters, thus deluded,
To venge themselves on Hermes have concluded
That Midas' brood* shall sit in Honour's chair,
To which the Muses' sons are only heir;
And fruitful wits that in aspiring are
Shall, discontent, run into regions far;
And few great lords in virtuous deeds shall joy,
But be surpris'd with every garish toy;   480

And still enrich the lofty servile clown,
Who with encroaching guile keeps Learning down.
Then muse not Cupid's suit no better sped,
Seeing in their loves the Fates were injured.

Second Sestiad

By this, sad Hero, with love unacquainted,
Viewing Leander's face, fell down and fainted.
He kiss'd her and breath'd life into her lips,
Wherewith as one displeas'd away she trips.
Yet as she went, full often look'd behind,
And many poor excuses did she find
To linger by the way, and once she stay'd
And would have turn'd again, but was afraid,
In offering parley, to be counted light.
So on she goes, and in her idle flight,   10
Her painted fan of curled plumes let fall,
Thinking to train Leander therewithal.
He, being a novice, knew not what she meant,
But stay'd, and after her a letter sent,
Which joyful Hero answer'd in such sort
As he had hope to scale the beauteous fort
Wherein the liberal graces lock'd their wealth,
And therefore to her tower he got by stealth.
Wide open stood the door, he need not climb;
And she herself before the 'pointed time   20
Had spread the board, with roses strew'd the room,
And oft look'd out, and mus'd he did not come.
At last he came; O! who can tell the greeting
These greedy lovers had at their first meeting.
He ask'd, she gave, and nothing was denied;
Both to each other quickly were affied.
Look how their hands, so were their hearts united,
And what he did she willingly requited.
Sweet are the kisses, the embracements sweet,
When like desires and affections meet;   30
For from the earth to heaven is Cupid rais'd,
Where fancy is in equal balance peis'd.
Yet she this rashness suddenly repented,
And turn'd aside, and to herself lamented,

As if her name and honour had been wrong'd
By being possess'd of him for whom she long'd;
Ay, and she wish'd, albeit not from her heart,
That he would leave her turret and depart.
The mirthful god of amorous pleasure smil'd
To see how he this captive nymph beguil'd;   40
For hitherto he did but fan the fire,
And kept it down that it might mount the higher.
Now wax'd she jealous lest his love abated,
Fearing her own thoughts made her to be hated.
Therefore unto him hastily she goes,
And like light Salmacis, her body throws
Upon his bosom, where with yielding eyes
She offers up herself a sacrifice,
To slake his anger if he were displeas'd.
O! what god would not therewith be appeas'd?   50
Like Aesop's cock,* this jewel he enjoy'd,
And as a brother with his sister toy'd,
Supposing nothing else was to be done,
Now he her favour and good will had won.
But know you not that creatures wanting sense
By nature have a mutual appetence,
And wanting organs to advance a step,
Mov'd by love's force, unto each other leap?
Much more in subjects having intellect
Some hidden influence breeds like effect.   60
Albeit Leander, rude in love and raw,
Long dallying with Hero, nothing saw
That might delight him more, yet he suspected
Some amorous rites or other were neglected.
Therefore unto his body hers he clung;
She, fearing on the rushes to be flung,
Striv'd with redoubl'd strength; the more she striv'd,
The more a gentle pleasing heat reviv'd,
Which taught him all that elder lovers know;
And now the same 'gan so to scorch and glow,   70
As in plain terms, yet cunningly, he crav'd it;
Love always makes those eloquent that have it.
She, with a kind of granting, put him by it,
And ever as he thought himself most nigh it,
Like to the tree of Tantalus she fled,

And, seeming lavish, sav'd her maidenhead.
Ne'er king more sought to keep his diadem,
Than Hero this inestimable gem.
Above our life we love a steadfast friend,
Yet when a token of great worth we send,   80
We often kiss it, often look thereon,
And stay the messenger that would be gone;
No marvel then though Hero would not yield
So soon to part from that she dearly held.
Jewels being lost are found again, this never;
'Tis lost but once, and once lost, lost for ever.

   Now had the Morn espi'd her lover's steeds,
Whereat she starts, puts on her purple weeds,
And, red for anger that he stay'd so long,
All headlong throws herself the clouds among.   90
And now Leander, fearing to be miss'd,
Embrac'd her suddenly, took leave, and kiss'd.
Long was he taking leave, and loth to go,
And kiss'd again, as lovers use to do.
Sad Hero wrung him by the hand and wept,
Saying, 'Let your vows and promises be kept.'
Then, standing at the door, she turn'd about,
As loth to see Leander going out.
And now the sun that through the' horizon peeps,
As pitying these lovers, downward creeps,   100
So that in silence of the cloudy night,
Though it was morning, did he take his flight.
But what the secret trusty night conceal'd,
Leander's amorous habit soon reveal'd;
With Cupid's myrtle was his bonnet crown'd,
About his arms the purple riband* wound,
Wherewith she wreath'd her largely spreading hair;
Nor could the youth abstain, but he must wear
The sacred ring wherewith he was endow'd
When first religious chastity she vow'd;   110
Which made his love through Sestos to be known,
And thence unto Abydos sooner blown
Than he could sail; for incorporeal Fame,
Whose weight consists in nothing but her name,
Is swifter than the wind, whose tardy plumes
Are reeking water and dull earthly fumes.

Home when he came, he seem'd not to be there,
But like exil'd air thrust from his sphere,
Set in a foreign place; and straight from thence,
Alcides-like, by mighty violence   120
He would have chas'd away the swelling main,
That him from her unjustly did detain.
Like as the sun in a diameter
Fires and inflames objects removed far,
And heateth kindly, shining laterally,
So beauty sweetly quickens when 'tis nigh,
But being separated and remov'd,
Burns where it cherish'd, murders where it lov'd.
Therefore even as an index to a book,
So to his mind was young Leander's look.   130
O! none but gods have power their love to hide;
Affection by the countenance is descried.
The light of hidden fire itself discovers,
And love that is conceal'd betrays poor lovers.
His secret flame apparently was seen;
Leander's father knew where he had been,
And for the same mildly rebuk'd his son,
Thinking to quench the sparkles new begun.
But love, resisted once, grows passionate,
And nothing more than counsel lovers hate;   140
For as a hot proud horse highly disdains
To have his head controll'd, but breaks the reins,
Spits forth the ringled bit, and with his hooves
Checks the submissive ground, so he that loves,
The more he is retrain'd, the worse he fares.
What is it now but mad Leander dares?
'O Hero, Hero!' thus he cried full oft,
And then he got him to a rock aloft,
Where having spi'd her tower, long star'd he on 't,
And pray'd the narrow toiling Hellespont   150
To part in twain, that he might come and go;
But still the rising billows answer'd 'No'.
With that he stripp'd him to the ivory skin,
And crying, 'Love, I come', leap'd lively in.
Whereat that sapphire-visag'd god* grew proud,
And made his capering Triton sound aloud,
Imagining that Ganymede, displeas'd,

Had left the heavens; therefore on him he seiz'd.
Leander striv'd; the waves about him wound,
And pull'd him to the bottom, where the ground   160
Was strew'd with pearl, and in low coral groves
Sweet singing mermaids sported with their loves
On heaps of heavy gold, and took great pleasure
To spurn in careless sort the shipwreck treasure:
For here the stately azure palace stood
Where kingly Neptune and his train abode.
The lusty god embrac'd him, call'd him love,
And swore he never should return to Jove.
But when he knew it was not Ganymede,
For under water he was almost dead,   170
He heav'd him up, and looking on his face,
Beat down the bold waves with his triple mace,
Which mounted up, intending to have kiss'd him,
And fell in drops like tears, because they miss'd him.
Leander, being up, began to swim,
And looking back, saw Neptune follow him;
Whereat aghast, the poor soul 'gan to cry:
'O! let me visit Hero ere I die!'
The god put Helle's bracelet on his arm,
And swore the sea should never do him harm.   180
He clapp'd his plump cheeks, with his tresses play'd,
And smiling wantonly, his love bewray'd.
He watch'd his arms, and as they open'd wide,
At every stroke betwixt them would he slide,
And steal a kiss, and then run out and dance,
And as he turn'd, cast many a lustful glance,
And throw him gaudy toys to please his eye,
And dive into the water, and there pry
Upon his breast, his thighs, and every limb,
And up again, and close behind him swim,   190
And talk of love. Leander made reply:
'You are deceiv'd, I am no woman, I.'
Thereat smil'd Neptune, and then told a tale,
How that a shepherd, sitting in a vale,
Play'd with a boy so lovely fair and kind
As for his love both earth and heaven pin'd;
That of the cooling river durst not drink
Lest water-nymphs should pull him from the brink;

And when he sported in the fragrant lawns,
Goat-footed satyrs and up-staring fauns
Would steal him thence. Ere half this tale was done,   200
'Ay me!' Leander cried, 'th' enamour'd sun,
That now should shine on Thetis' glassy bower,
Descends upon my radiant Hero's tower.
O! that these tardy arms of mine were wings!'
And as he spake, upon the waves he springs.
Neptune was angry that he gave no ear,
And in his heart revenging malice bare
He flung at him his mace; but as it went
He call'd it in, for love made him repent.   210
The mace returning back his own hand hit,
As meaning to be veng'd for darting it.
When this fresh-bleeding wound Leander view'd,
His colour went and came, as if he rued
The grief which Neptune felt. In gentle breasts
Relenting thoughts, remorse, and pity rests;
And who have hard hearts and obdurate minds
But vicious, hare-brain'd and illiterate hinds?
The god, seeing him with pity to be mov'd,
Thereon concluded that he was belov'd.   220
(Love is too full of faith, too credulous,
With folly and false hope deluding us.)
Wherefore, Leander's fancy to surprise,
To the rich ocean for gifts he flies.
'Tis wisdom to give much; a gift prevails
When deep persuading oratory fails.
By this, Leander being near the land
Cast down his weary feet, and felt the sand.
Breathless albeit he were, he rested not
Till to the solitary tower he got,   230
And knock'd and call'd, at which celestial noise
The longing heart of Hero much more joys
Than nymphs or shepherds when the timbrel rings,
Or crooked dolphin when the sailor sings.
She stay'd not for her robes, but straight arose,
And drunk with gladness, to the door she goes;
Where seeing a naked man, she screech'd for fear,
(Such sights as this to tender maids are rare)
And ran into the dark herself to hide.

Rich jewels in the dark are soonest spied.   240
Unto her was he led, or rather drawn,
By those white limbs which sparkl'd through the lawn.
The nearer that he came, the more she fled,
And seeking refuge, slipp'd into her bed.
Whereon Leander sitting, thus began,
Through numbing cold all feeble, faint, and wan:
'If not for love, yet, love, for pity sake,
Me in thy bed and maiden bosom take;
At least vouchsafe these arms some little room,
Who, hoping to embrace thee, cheerly swum;   250
This head was beat with many a churlish billow,
And therefore let it rest upon thy pillow.'
Herewith affrighted, Hero shrunk away,
And in her lukewarm place Leander lay,
Whose lively heat, like fire from heaven fet,
Would animate gross clay, and higher set
The drooping thoughts of base-declining souls,
Than dreary Mars carousing nectar bowls.
His hands he cast upon her like a snare:
She, overcome with shame and sallow fear,   260
Like chaste Diana, when Actaeon spied her,
Being suddenly betray'd, div'd down to hide her;
And as her silver body downward went,
With both her hands she made the bed a tent,
And in her own mind thought herself secure,
O'ercast with dim and darksome coverture.
And now she lets him whisper in her ear,
Flatter, entreat, promise, protest, and swear;
Yet ever as he greedily assay'd
To touch those dainties, she the Harpy play'd,   270
And every limb did, as a soldier stout,
Defend the fort and keep the foeman out.
For though the rising ivory mount he scal'd,
Which is with azure-circling lines empal'd,
Much like a globe (a globe may I term this,
By which love sails to regions full of bliss),
Yet there with Sisyphus he toil'd in vain,
Till gentle parley did the truce obtain.
Wherein Leander on her quivering breast
Breathless spoke something, and sigh'd out the rest;   280

Which so prevail'd as he with small ado
Enclos'd her in his arms and kiss'd her too.
And every kiss to her was as a charm,
And to Leander as a fresh alarm,
So that the truce was broke, and she, alas!
Poor silly maiden, at his mercy was.
Love is not full of pity, as men say,
But deaf and cruel where he means to prey.
Even as a bird, which in our hands we wring,
Forth plungeth and oft flutters with her wing,   290
She trembling strove; this strife of hers, like that
Which made the world, another world begat
Of unknown joy. Treason was in her thought,
And cunningly to yield herself she sought.
Seeming not won, yet won she was at length;
In such wars women use but half their strength.
Leander now, like Theban Hercules
Enter'd the orchard of th' Hesperides,
Whose fruit none rightly can describe but he
That pulls or shakes it from the golden tree.   300
And now she wish'd this night were never done,
And sigh'd to think upon th' approaching sun;
For much it grieve'd her that the bright daylight
Should know the pleasure of this blessed night,
And them like Mars and Erycine display,
Both in each other's arms chained as they lay.
Again she knew not how to frame her look,
Or speak to him who in a moment took
That which so long so charily she kept;
And fain by stealth away she would have crept,   310
And to some corner secretly have gone,
Leaving Leander in the bed alone.
But as her naked feet were whipping out,
He on the sudden cling'd her so about
That mermaid-like unto the floor she slid,
One half appear'd, the other half was hid.
Thus near the bed she blushing stood upright,
And from her countenance behold ye might
A kind of twilight break, which through the hair,
As from an orient cloud, glims here and there;   320
And round about the chamber this false morn

Brought forth the day before the day was born.
So Hero's ruddy cheek Hero betray'd,
And her all naked to his sight display'd;
Whence his admiring eyes more pleasure took
Than Dis on heaps of gold fixing his look.
By this, Apollo's golden harp began
To sound forth music to the ocean;
Which watchful Hesperus no sooner heard
But he the day's bright-bearing car prepar'd,   330
And ran before, as harbinger of light,
And with his flaring beams mock'd ugly Night
Till she, o'ercome with anguish, shame and rage,
Dang'd down to hell her loathsome carriage.

Desunt nonnulla

Francis Beaumont

I sing the fortune of a luckless pair,
Whose spotless souls now in one body be,
For beauty still is prodromus* to care,
Cross'd by the sad stars of nativity;
And of the strange enchantment of a well,
Given by the gods, my sportive Muse doth write,
Which sweet-lipp'd Ovid long ago did tell,
Wherein who bathes, straight turns hermaphrodite:
   I hope my poem is so lively writ,
   That thou wilt turn half-maid with reading it.

Salmacis and Hermaphroditus
(1602)

My wanton lines do treat of amorous love,
Such as would bow the hearts of gods above.
Then, Venus, thou great Cytheraean queen,
That hourly tripp'st on the Idalian green,
Thou, laughing Erycina, deign to see
These verses wholly consecrate to thee;
Temper them so within thy Paphian shrine,
That every lover's eye may melt a line;
Command the god of love, that little king,
To give each verse a slight touch with his wing,   10
That, as I write, one line may draw the other,
And every word skip nimbly o'er another.
   There was a lovely boy the nymphs had kept,
That on th' Idalian mountains oft had slept,
Begot and born by powers that dwelt above,
By learnèd Mercury of the queen of love.*
A face he had that shew'd his parents' fame,
And from them both conjoin'd he drew his name.
So wondrous fair he was, that (as they say)

Diana being hunting on a day,   20
She saw the boy upon a green bank lay him,
And there the virgin huntress meant to slay him,
Because no nymphs would now pursue the chase,
For all were struck blind with the wanton's face.
But when that beauteous face Diana saw,
Her arms were numbèd, and she could not draw:
Yet did she strive to shoot, but all in vain,
She bent her bow, and loos'd it straight again.
Then she began to chide her wanton eye,
And fain would shoot, but durst not see him die: 30
She turn'd and shot, but did of purpose miss him;
She turn'd again, and did of purpose kiss him.
Then the boy ran; for (some say) had he stay'd,
Diana had no longer been a maid.
Phoebus so doted on this roseate face,
That he hath oft stole closely from his place,
When he did lie by fair Leucothoë's side,
To dally with him in the vales of Ide;
And ever since this lovely boy did die,
Phoebus each day about the world doth fly,   40
And on the earth he seeks him all the day,
And every night he seeks him in the sea.
His cheek was sanguine, and his lip as red,
As are the blushing leaves of the rose spread;
And I have heard that, till this boy was born,
Roses grew white upon the virgin thorn;
Till one day walking to a pleasant spring,
To hear how cunningly the birds could sing,
Laying him down upon a flowery bed,
The roses blush'd, and turn'd themselves to red: 50
The rose that blush'd not, for his great offence
The gods did punish, and for impudence
They gave this doom, that was agreed by all,
The smell of the white rose should be but small.
His hair was bushy, but it was not long;
The nymphs had done his tresses mighty wrong,
For, as it grew, they pull'd away his hair,
And made habiliments of gold to wear.
His eyes were Cupid's, for, until his birth,
Cupid had eyes, and liv'd upon the earth;   60

Till on a day, when the great queen of love
Was by her white doves drawn from heaven above
Unto the top of the Idalian hill,
To see how well the nymphs her charge fulfil,
And whether they had done the goddess right
In nursing of her sweet Hermaphrodite;
Whom when she saw, although complete and full,
Yet she complain'd his eyes were somewhat dull;
And therefore, more the wanton boy to grace,
She pull'd the sparkling eyes from Cupid's face,   70
Feigning a cause to take away his sight,
Because the ape would sometimes shoot for spite:
But Venus set those eyes in such a place,
As grac'd those clear eyes with a clearer face.
For his white hand each goddess did him woo,
For it was whiter than the driven snow;
His leg was straighter than the thigh of Jove,
And he far fairer than the god of love.*
    When first this well-shap'd boy, beauty's chief king,
Had seen the labour of the fifteenth spring,   80
How curiously it painted all the earth,
He 'gan to travel from his place of birth,
Leaving the stately hills where he was nurst,
And where the nymphs had brought him up at first.
He love'd to travel unto coasts unknown,
To see the regions far beyond his own,
Seeking clear watery springs to bathe him in,
(For he did love to wash his ivory skin).
The lovely nymphs have oft times seen him swim,
And closely stole his clothes from off the brim,   90
Because the wanton wenches would so fain
See him come nak'd to ask his clothes again.
He love'd besides to see the Lycian grounds,
And know the wealthy Carians' utmost bounds.
    Using to travel thus, one day he found
A crystal brook that trill'd along the ground;
A brook that in reflection did surpass
The clear reflection of the clearest glass.
About the side there grew no foggy reeds,
Nor was the fount compass'd with barren weeds,   100
But living turf grew all along the side,

And grass that ever flourish'd in his pride.
Within this brook a beauteous nymph did dwell,
Who for her comely feature did excel:
So fair she was, of such a pleasing grace,
So straight a body, and so sweet a face,
So soft a belly, such a lusty thigh,
So large a forehead, such a crystal eye,
So soft and moist a hand, so smooth a breast,
So fair a cheek, so well in all the rest,   110
That Jupiter would revel in her bower,
Were he to spend again his golden shower;
Her teeth were whiter than the morning's milk,
Her lip was softer than the softest silk;
Her hair as far surpass'd the burnish'd gold,
As silver doth excel the basest mold.
Jove courted her for her translucent eye,
And told her he would place her in the sky;
Promising her, if she would be his love,
He would engrave her in the heavens above;   120
Telling this lovely nymph, that, if he would,
He could deceive her in a shower of gold;*
Or, like a swan, come to her naked bed,*
And so deceive her of her maidenhead.
But yet, because he thought that pleasure best
Where each consenting joins each loving breast,
He would put off that all-commanding crown,
Whose terror stroke th' aspiring giants down;
That glittering crown, whose radiant sight did toss
Great Pelion from the top of mighty Oss,   130
He would depose from his world-swaying head,
To taste the amorous pleasure of her bed;
This added he besides, the more to grace her,
Like a bright star he would in heaven's vault place her.
By this the proud lascivious nymph was mov'd,
Perceiving by great Jove she was belov'd;
And, hoping as a star she should ere long
Be stern or gracious to the seaman's song,
(For mortals still are subject to the eye,
And what it sees they strive to get as high,)   140
She was contented that almighty Jove
Should have the first and best fruits of her love;

(For women may be liken'd to the year,
Whose first fruits still do make the daintiest cheer;)
But yet Astraea first should plight her troth
For the performance of Jove's sacred oath:
(Just times decline, and all good days are dead,
When heavenly oaths had need be warranted.)
   This heard great Jupiter, and lik'd it well,
And hastily he seeks Astraea's cell,   150
About the massy earth searching her tower:
But she had long since left this earthly bower,
And flew to heaven above, loathing to see
The sinful action of humanity.
Which when Jove did perceive, he left the earth,
And flew up to the place of his own birth,
The burning heavenly throne, where he did spy
Astraea's palace in the glittering sky.
This stately tower was builded up on high,
Far from the reach of any mortal eye;   160
And from the palace' side there did distil
A little water through a little quill,
The dew of justice, which did seldom fall,
And, when it dropt, the drops were very small.
Glad was great Jove when he beheld her tower,
Meaning a while to rest him in her bower,
And therefore sought to enter at her door:
But there was such a busy rout before
Some serving-men, and some promoters be,
That he could pass no foot without a fee;   170
But, as he goes, he reaches out his hands,
And pays each one in order as he stands,
And still as he was paying those before,
Some slipp'd again betwixt him and the door.
   At length (with much ado) he pass'd them all,
And entering straight into a spacious hall,
Full of dark angles and of hidden ways,
Crookèd meanders, infinite delays,
All which delays and entries he must pass
Ere he could come where just Astraea was;   180
All these being pass'd by his immortal wit,
Without her door he saw a porter sit,
An agèd man that long time there had been,

Who us'd to search all those that enter'd in,
And still to every one he gave this curse,
'None must see Justice but with empty purse.'
This man search'd Jove for his own private gain,
To have the money which did yet remain,
Which was but small, for much was spent before
On the tumultuous rout that kept the door: 190
When he had done, he brought him to the place,
Where he might see divine Astraea's face.
There the great king of gods and men in went,
And saw his daughter Venus there lament,
And crying loud for justice, whom Jove found
Kneeling before Astraea on the ground;
And still she cried and begg'd for a just doom
Against black Vulcan, that unseemly groom,
Whom she had chosen for her only love,
Though she was daughter to great thundering Jove;   200
And though the fairest goddess, yet content
To marry him, though weak and impotent.
But, for all this, they always were at strife;
For ever more he rail'd at her his wife,
Telling her still, 'Thou art no wife of mine,
Another's strumpet, Mars his concubine.'
By this, Astraea spied almighty Jove,
And bow'd her finger to the queen of love
To cease her suit, which she would hear anon,
When the great king of all the world was gone.   210
Then she descended from her stately throne,
Which seat was builded all of jasper stone,
And o'er the seat was painted all above
The wanton unseen stealths of amorous Jove:
There might a man behold the naked pride
Of lovely Venus in the vale of Ide,
When Pallas, and Jove's beauteous wife, and she,
Strove for the prize of beauty's rarity;
And there lame Vulcan and his Cyclops strove
To make the thunderbolts for mighty Jove.   220
From this same stately throne she down descended,
And said the griefs of Jove should be amended,
Asking the king of gods what luckless cause,
What great contempt of state, what breach of laws,

(For sure she thought some uncouth cause befell,
That made him visit poor Astraea's cell,)
Troubled his thought; and, if she might decide it,
Who vex'd great Jove full dearly should abide it.
Jove only thank'd her, and began to shew
His cause of coming, (for each one doth know   230
The longing words of lovers are not many,
If they desire to be enjoy'd of any,)
Telling Astraea, it would now befall
That she might make him blest that blesseth all;
For, as he walk'd upon the flowery earth,
To which his own hands whilom gave a birth,
To see how strait he held it, and how just
He rul'd this massy ponderous heap of dust;
He laid him down by a cool river side,
Whose pleasant water did so gently slide,   240
With such soft whispering, for the brook was deep,
That it had lull'd him in a heavenly sleep.
When first he laid him down, there was none near him,
(For he did call before, but none could hear him,)
But a fair nymph was bathing when he wak'd,
(Here sigh'd great Jove, and after brought forth) nak'd:
He seeing, lov'd the nymph; yet here did rest
Where just Astraea might make Jove be blest,
If she would pass her faithful word so far
As that great Jove should make the maid a star.   250
Astraea yielded; at which Jove was pleas'd,
And all his longing hopes and fears were eas'd.
Jove took his leave, and parted from her sight,
Whose thoughts were full of lovers' sweet delight;
And she ascended to the throne above,
To hear the griefs of the great queen of love:
But she was satisfied, and would no more
Rail at her husband as she did before;
But forth she tripp'd apace, because she strove
With her swift feet to overtake great Jove.   260
She skipp'd so nimbly as she went to look him,
That at the palace-door she overtook him.
The way was plain and broad as they went out,
And now they could see no tumultuous rout.
Here Venus, fearing lest the love of Jove

Should make this maid be plac'd in heaven above,
Because she thought this nymph so wondrous bright
That she would dazzle her accustom'd light,
And fearing now she should not first be seen
Of all the glittering stars as she had been,   270
But that the wanton nymph would every night
Be first that should salute each mortal sight,
Began to tell great Jove she griev'd to see
The heaven so full of his iniquity,
Complaining that each strumpet now was grac'd,
And with immortal goddesses was plac'd,
Entreating him to place in heaven no more
Each wanton strumpet and lascivious whore.

    Jove, mad with love, harken'd not what she said,
His thoughts were so entangled with the maid;   280
But furiously he to his palace lept,
Being minded there till morning to have slept;
For the next morn, so soon as Phoebus' rays
Should yet shine cool by reason of the seas,
And ere the parting tears of Thetis' bed
Should be quite shak'd from off his glittering head,
Astraea promis'd to attend great Jove
At his own palace in the heaven above,
And at that palace she would set her hand
To what the love-sick god should her command: 290
But to descend to earth she did deny;
She loath'd the sight of any mortal eye,
And, for the compass of the earthly round,
She would not set one foot upon the ground:
Therefore Jove meant to rise but with the sun,
Yet thought it long until the night was done.

    In the mean space Venus was drawn along,
By her white doves, unto the sweating throng
Of hammering blacksmiths, at the lofty hill
Of stately Etna,* whose top burneth still;   300
(For at that burning mountain's glittering top
Her cripple husband Vulcan kept his shop.)
To him she went, and so collogues that night*
With the best strains of pleasure's sweet delight,
That, ere they parted, she made Vulcan swear
By dreadful Styx (an oath that gods do fear),

If Jove would make the mortal maid a star,
Himself should frame his instruments of war:
He took his oath by black Cocytus' lake,
He never more a thunderbolt would make;   310
For Venus so this night his senses pleas'd,
That now he thought his former griefs were eas'd:
She with her hands the blacksmith's body bound
And with her ivory arms she twin'd him round;
And still the fair queen with a pretty grace
Dispers'd her sweet breath o'er his swarthy face;
Her snowy arms so well she did display,
That Vulcan thought they melted as they lay.
Until the morn in this delight they lay,
Then up they got, and hasted fast away,   320
In the white chariot of the queen of love,
Towards the palace of great thundering Jove;
Where they did see divine Astraea stand,
To pass her word for what Jove should command.
In limp'd the blacksmith; after stept his queen,
Whose light arrayment was of lovely green.
When they were in, Vulcan began to swear
By oaths that Jupiter himself doth fear,
If any whore in heaven's bright vault were seen
To dim the shining of his beauteous queen,   330
Each mortal man should the great gods disgrace,
And mock almighty Jove unto his face;
And giants should enforce bright heaven to fall,
Ere he would frame one thunderbolt at all.
Jove did entreat him that he would forbear:
The more he spake, the more did Vulcan swear.
Jove heard the words, and 'gan to make his moan,
That mortal men would pluck him from his throne,
Or else he must incur this plague, he said,
Quite to forego the pleasure of the maid;   340
And once he thought, rather than lose her blisses,
Her heavenly sweets, her most delicious kisses,
Her soft embraces, and the amorous nights
That he should often spend in her delights,
He would be quite thrown down by mortal hands
From the blest place where his bright palace stands:
But afterwards he saw with better sight,

He should be scorn'd by every mortal wight,
If he should want his thunderbolts to beat
Aspiring mortals from his glittering seat;   350
Therefore the god no more did woo or move her,
But left to seek her love, though not to love her:
Yet he forgot not that he woo'd the lass,
But made her twice as beauteous as she was,
Because his wonted love he needs would shew.
This have I heard, but yet scarce thought it true;
And whether her clear beauty was so bright
That it could dazzle the immortal sight
Of gods, and make them for her love despair,
I do not know, but, sure, the maid was fair.   360
Yet the fair nymph was never seen resort
Unto the savage and the bloody sport
Of chaste Diana, nor was ever wont
To bend a bow, nor ever did she hunt;
Nor did she ever strive with pretty cunning
To overgo her fellow nymphs in running;
For she was the fair water-nymph alone
That unto chaste Diana was unknown.
It is reported that her fellows us'd
To bid her (though the beauteous nymph refus'd)   370
To take a painted quiver or a dart,
And put her lazy idleness apart:
But in her crystal fountain oft she swims,
Where oft she washes o'er her snowy limbs:
Sometimes she comb'd her soft dishevell'd hair,
Which with a fillet tied she oft did wear;
But sometimes loose she let it hang behind,
When she was pleas'd to grace the eastern wind,
For up and down it would her tresses hurl,
And, as she went, it made her loose hair curl: 380
Oft in the water did she look* her face,
And oft she us'd to practise what quaint grace
Might well become her, and what comely feature
Might be best fitting so divine a creature.
Her skin was with a thin veil overthrown,
Through which her naked beauty clearly shone;
She us'd in this light raiment, as she was,
To spread her body on the dewy grass:

Sometimes, by her own fountain as she walks,
She nips the flowers from off the fertile stalks,   390
And with a garland of the sweating vine
Sometimes she doth her beauteous front entwine.
But she was gathering flowers with her white hand,
When she beheld Hermaphroditus stand
By her clear fountain, wondering at the sight,
That there was any brook could be so bright;
For this was the bright river where the boy
Did die himself, that he could not enjoy
Himself in pleasure, nor could taste the blisses
Of his own melting and delicious kisses.   400
Here did she see him, and by Venus' law
She did desire to have him as she saw.
        But the fair nymph had never seen the place
Where the boy was, nor his enchanting face,
But by an uncouth accident of love
Betwixt great Phoebus and the son of Jove,
Light-headed Bacchus; for, upon a day,
As the boy-god was keeping on his way,
Bearing his vine-leaves and his ivy-bands
To Naxos, where his house and temple stands,   410
He saw the nymph, and, seeing, he did stay,
And threw his leaves and ivy-bands away,
Thinking at first she was of heavenly birth,
Some goddess that did live upon the earth;
Virgin Diana that so lovely shone
When she did court her sweet Endymion:
But he, a god, at last did plainly see
She had no mark of immortality.
Unto the nymph went the young god of wine,
Whose head was chaf'd so with the bleeding vine   420
That now or fear or terror had he none,
But 'gan to court her as she sat alone.
'Fairer than fairest,' (thus began his speech,)
'Would but your radiant eye please to enrich
My eye with looking, or one glance to give
Whereby my other parts may feed and live,
Or with one sight my senses to inspire
Far livelier than the stoln Promethean fire,
Then might I live; then by the sunny light

That should proceed from thy thrice radiant sight,   430
I might survive to ages: but that missing,' –
(At that same word he would have fain been kissing) –
'I pine, fair nymph: oh, never let me die
For one poor glance from thy translucent eye,
Far more transparent than the clearest brook!'
The nymph was taken with his golden hook;
Yet she turn'd back, and would have tripp'd away,
But Bacchus forc'd the lovely maid to stay,
Asking her why she struggled to be gone,
Why such a nymph should wish to live alone?   440
Heaven never made her fair that she should vaunt
She kept all beauty, it would never grant
She should be born so beauteous from her mother,
But to reflect her beauty on another:
'Then with a sweet kiss cast thy beams on me,
And I'll reflect them back again on thee.
At Naxos stands my temple and my shrine,
Where I do press the lusty swelling vine;
There with the green ivy shall thy head be bound,
And with the red grape be encircled round;   450
There shall Silenus sing unto thy praise
His drunken reeling songs and tippling lays.
Come hither, gentle nymph.' Here blush'd the maid,
And fain she would have gone, but yet she stay'd.
Bacchus perceiv'd he had o'ercome the lass,
And down he throws her in the dewy grass,
And kiss'd the helpless nymph upon the ground,
And would have stray'd beyond that lawful bound.
    This saw bright Phoebus, for his glittering eye
Sees all that lies below the starry sky;   460
And, for an old affection that he bore
Unto this lovely nymph long time before
(For he would oft times in his circle stand,
And sport himself upon her snowy hand).
He kept her from the sweets of Bacchus' bed,
And 'gainst her will he sav'd her maidenhead.
Bacchus, perceiving this, apace did hie
Unto the palace of swift Mercury;
But he did find him, far below his birth,
Drinking with thieves and catchpoles* on the earth,   470

And they were parting what they stole to-day,
In consultation for to-morrow's prey.
To him went youthful Bacchus, and begun
To shew his cause of grief against the Sun;
How he bereft him of his heavenly blisses,
His sweet delight, his nectar-flowing kisses,
And other sweeter sweets that he had won
But for the malice of the bright-fac'd Sun;
Entreating Mercury, by all the love
That had been borne amongst the sons of Jove   480
(Of which they two were part), to stand his friend
Against the god that did him so offend.
The quaint-tongu'd issue of great Atlas' race,
Swift Mercury, that with delightful grace,
And pleasing accents of his feignèd tongue,
Hath oft reform'd a rude uncivil throng
Of mortals; that great messenger of Jove
And all the meaner gods that dwell above;
He whose acute wit was so quick and sharp
In the invention of the crookèd harp;   490
He that's so cunning with his jesting slights
To steal from heavenly gods or earthly wights, –
Bearing a great hate in his grievèd breast
Against that great commander of the west,
Bright-fac'd Apollo; for upon a day
Young Mercury did steal his beasts away;
Which the great god perceiving, straight did shew
The piercing arrows and the fearful bow
That kill'd great Python, and with that did threat him
To bring his beasts again, or he would beat him;   500
Which Mercury perceiving, unespied
Did closely steal his arrows from his side:
For this old grudge he was the easier won
To help young Bacchus 'gainst the fiery Sun.
  And now the Sun was in the middle way,
And had o'ercome the one half of the day,
Scorching so hot upon the reeking sand
That lies upon the near Egyptian land,
That the hot people, burnt even from their birth,
Do creep again into their mother Earth;   510
When Mercury did take his powerful wand,

His charming caduceus in his hand,
And the thick beaver which he us'd to wear,
When aught from Jove he to the Sun did bear,
That did protect him from the piercing light
Which did proceed from Phoebus' glittering sight:
Clad in these powerful ornaments he flies
With out-stretch'd wings up to the azure skies,
Where seeing Phoebus in his orient shine,
He did so well revenge the god of wine   520
That, whilst the Sun wonders his chariot reels,
The crafty god had stoln away his wheels:
Which when he did perceive, he down did slide
(Laying his glittering coronet aside)
From the bright spangled firmament above,
To seek the nymph that Bacchus so did love,
And found her looking in her watery glass,
To see how clear her radiant beauty was;
And, for he had but little time to stay,
Because he meant to finish out his day,   530
At the first sight he 'gan to make his moan,
Telling her how his fiery wheels were gone;
Promising her, if she would but obtain
The wheels, that Mercury had stoln, again,
That he might end his day, she should enjoy
The heavenly sight of the most beauteous boy
That ever was. The nymph was pleas'd with this,
Hoping to reap some unaccustom'd bliss
By the sweet pleasure that she should enjoy
In the blest sight of such a melting boy: 540
Therefore at his request she did obtain
The burning wheels, that he had lost, again;
Which when he had receiv'd, he left the land,
And brought them thither where his coach did stand,
And there he set them on, for all this space
The horses had not stirr'd from out their place;
Which when he saw, he wept, and 'gan to say,
'Would Mercury had stoln my wheels away
When Phaëton, my hair-brain'd issue, tried
What a laborious thing it was to guide   550
My burning chariot! then he might have pleas'd me,
And of a father's grief he might have eas'd me;

For then the steeds would have obey'd his will,
Or else at least they would have rested still.'
When he had done, he took his whip of steel,
Whose bitter smart he made his horses feel;
For he did lash so hard to end the day,
That he was quickly at the western sea:
And there with Thetis did he rest a space,
For he did never rest in any place   560
Before that time; but ever since his wheels
Were stoln away, his burning chariot reels
Tow'rds the declining of the parting day;
Therefore he lights, and mends them in the sea:
And though the poets feign that Jove did make
A treble night for fair Alcmena's* sake,
That he might sleep securely with his love,
Yet, sure, the long night was unknown to Jove:
But the Sun's wheels one day disorder'd more,
Were thrice as long a-mending as before.   570
Now was the Sun environ'd with the sea,
Cooling his watery tresses as he lay,
And in dread Neptune's kingdom while he sleeps,
Fair Thetis clips him in the watery deeps;
There mermaids and the Tritons of the west,
Straining their voices to make Titan rest.
And while the black Night, with her pitchy hand,
Took just possession of the swarthy land.
He spent the darksome hours in this delight,
Giving his power up to the gladsome Night;   580
For ne'er before he was so truly blest
To take an hour or one poor minute's rest.
But now the burning god this pleasure feels
By reason of his newly-crazèd wheels:
There must he stay until lame Vulcan send
The fiery wheels which he had took to mend.
   Now all the night the smith so hard had wrought,
That, ere the Sun could wake, his wheels were brought.
Titan being pleas'd with rest and not to rise,
And loath to open yet his slumbering eyes,   590
And yet perceiving how the longing sight
Of mortals waited for his glittering light,
He sent Aurora from him to the sky

To give a glimpsing to each mortal eye.
Aurora, much asham'd of that same place
That great Apollo's light was wont to grace,
Finding no place to hide her shameful head,
Painted her chaste cheeks with a blushing red;
Which ever since remain'd upon her face
In token of her new-receiv'd disgrace: 600
Therefore she not so white as she had been,
Loathing of every mortal to be seen,
No sooner can the rosy-finger'd Morn
Kiss every flower that by her dew is born,
But from the golden window she doth peep
When the most part of earthly creatures sleep.
By this, bright Titan open'd had his eyes,
And 'gan to jerk his horses through the skies,
And, taking in his hand his fiery whip,
He made Eous and swift Aethon skip   610
So fast, that straight he dazzled had the sight
Of fair Aurora, glad to see his light.
      And now the Sun in all his fiery haste
Did call to mind his promise lately past,
And all the vows and oaths that he did pass
Unto fair Salmacis, the beauteous lass;
For he had promis'd her she should enjoy
So lovely, fair, and such a well-shap'd boy,
As ne'er before his own all-seeing eye
Saw from his bright seat in the starry sky.   620
Remembering this, he sent the boy that way
Where the clear fountain of the fair nymph lay;
There was he come to seek some pleasing brook.
No sooner came he but the nymph was strook;
And though she longèd to embrace the boy,
Yet did the nymph a while defer her joy,
Till she had bound up her loose flagging hair,
And order'd well the garments she did wear,
Feigning her countenance with a lover's care,
And did deserve to be accounted fair;   630
When thus much spake she while the boy abode,
'O boy, most worthy to be thought a god!
Thou mayst inhabit in the glorious place
Of gods, or mayst proceed from human race;

Thou mayst be Cupid, or the god of wine
That lately woo'd me with the swelling vine:
But whatso'er thou art, oh, happy he
That was so blest to be a sire to thee!
Thy happy mother is most blest of many;
Blessèd thy sisters, if her womb bare any;   640
Both fortunate, and, oh, thrice happy she
Whose too much blessèd breasts gave suck to thee!
If any's wish with thy sweet bed be blest,
Oh, she is far more happy than the rest!
If thou hast any, let my sport be stol'n,
Or else let me be she, if thou hast none.'
Here did she pause a while, and then she said,
'Be not obdurate to a silly maid:
A flinty heart within a snowy breast
Is like base mold lock'd in a golden chest: 650
They say the eye's the index of the heart,
And shews th' affection of each inward part:
Then love plays lively there, the little god*
Hath a clear crystal palace of abode;
Oh, bar him not from playing in thy heart,
That sports himself upon each outward part!'
Thus much she spake, and then her tongue was hush'd.
At her loose speech Hermaphroditus blush'd;
He knew not what love was, yet love did shame him,
Making him blush, and yet his blush became him: 660
Then might a man his shamefast colour see
Like the ripe apple on a sunny tree,
Or ivory dy'd o'er with a pleasing red,
Or like the pale morn being shadowèd.
By this, the nymph recover'd had her tongue,
That, to her thinking, lay in silence long,
And said, 'Thy cheek is mild: oh, be thou so!
Thy cheek saith, ay; then do not answer, no;
Thy cheek doth shame; then do thou shame,' she said;
'It is a man's shame to deny a maid: 670
Thou look'st to sport with Venus in her tower,
And be belov'd of every heavenly power;
Men are but mortals, so are women too,
Why should your thoughts aspire more than ours do?
For, sure, they do aspire; else could a youth,

Whose countenance is full of spotless truth,
Be so relentless to a virgin's tongue?
Let me be woo'd by thee but half so long,
With half those terms do but my love require,
And I will easily grant thee thy desire: 680
Ages are bad when men become so slow,
That poor unskilful maids are forc'd to woo.'
    Her radiant beauty and her subtle art
So deeply struck Hermaphroditus' heart,
That she had won his love, but that the light
Of her translucent eyes did shine too bright;
For long he look'd upon the lovely maid,
And at the last Hermaphroditus said,
'How should I love thee, when I do espy
A far more beauteous nymph hid in thy eye?   690
When thou dost love, let not that nymph be nigh thee,
Nor, when thou woo'st, let that same nymph be by thee;
Or quite obscure her from thy lover's face,
Or hide her beauty in a darker place.'
By this the nymph perceiv'd he did espy
None but himself reflected in her eye;
And, for himself no more she meant to shew him,
She shut her eyes, and blindfold thus did woo him;
'Fair boy, think not thy beauty can dispense
With any pain due to a bad offence;   700
Remember how the gods punish'd that boy
That scorn'd to let a beauteous nymph enjoy
Her long-wish'd pleasure; for the peevish elf.
Lov'd of all others, needs would love himself:*
So mayst thou love, perhaps thou mayst be blest
By granting to a luckless nymph's request;
Then rest a while with me amidst these weeds:
The Sun, that sees all, sees not lovers' deeds;
Phoebus is blind when love-sports are begun,
And never sees until their sports be done.   710
Believe me, boy, thy blood is very staid,
Thou art so loath to kiss a youthful maid:
Wert thou a maid and I a man, I'll shew thee
With what a manly boldness I could woo thee;
"Fairer than love's queen," thus would I begin,
"Might not my over-boldness be a sin,

I would entreat this favour, if I could,
Thy roseate cheeks a little to behold!"
Then would I beg a touch, and then a kiss,
And then a lower, yet a higher, bliss;   720
Then would I ask what Jove and Leda did,
When like a swan the crafty god was hid?
What came he for? why did he there abide?
Surely, I think he did not come to chide;
He came to see her face, to talk and chat,
To touch, to kiss: came he for nought but that?
Yes, something else: what was it he would have?
That which all men of maidens ought to crave.'
    This said, her eyelids wide she did display,
But in this space the boy was run away;   730
The wanton speeches of the lovely lass
Forc'd him for shame to hide him in the grass.
When she perceiv'd she could not see him near her,
When she had call'd, and yet he would not hear her;
Look, how, when Autumn comes, a little space
Paleth the red blush of the Summer's face,
Tearing the leaves, the Summer's covering,
Three months in weaving by the curious Spring,
Making the grass, his green locks, go to wrack,
Tearing each ornament from off his back;   740
So did she spoil the garments she did wear,
Tearing whole ounces of her golden hair.
She thus deluded of her longèd bliss,
With much ado at last she utter'd this;
'Why wert thou bashful, boy? thou hast no part
Shews thee to be of such a female heart.
His eye is grey; so is the Morning's eye,
That blusheth always when the day is nigh:
Then his grey eye's the cause? that cannot be,
The grey-ey'd Morn is far more bold than he,   750
For with a gentle dew from Heaven's bright tower,
It gets the maidenhead of every flower:
I would to God he were the roseate Morn,
And I a flower from out the earth new-born!
His face is smooth; Narcissus' face was so,
And he was careless of a sad nymph's woe:
Then that's the cause; and yet that cannot be;

Youthful Narcissus was more bold than he,
Because he died for love, though of his shade;
This boy nor loves himself, nor yet a maid.   760
Besides, his glorious eye is wondrous bright;
So is the fiery and all-seeing light
Of Phoebus, who at every morning's birth
Blusheth for shame upon the sullen earth:
Then that's the cause; and yet that cannot be;
The fiery Sun is far more bold than he;
He nightly kisseth Thetis in the sea;
All know the story of Leucothoë.
His cheek is red; so is the fragrant rose,
Whose ruddy cheek with over-blushing glows: 770
Then that's the cause; and yet that cannot be;
Each blushing rose is far more bold than he;
Whose boldness may be plainly seen in this,
The ruddy rose is not asham'd to kiss;
For always, when the day is new begun,
The spreading rose will kiss the morning sun.'
   This said, hid in the grass she did espy him,
And, stumbling with her will, she fell down by him,
And with her wanton talk, because he woo'd not,
Begg'd that which he, poor novice, understood not;   780
And, for she could not get a greater bliss,
She did entreat at least a sister's kiss:
But still the more she did the boy beseech,
The more he pouted at her wanton speech.
At last the nymph began to touch his skin,
Whiter than mountain snow hath ever been,
And did in pureness that clear spring surpass
Wherein Actaeon saw th' Arcadian lass.*
Thus did she dally long, till at the last
In her white palm she lock'd his white hand fast;   790
Then in her hands his wrist she 'gan to close,
When through his pulses straight his warm blood glows,
Whose youthful music, fanning Cupid's fire,
In her warm breast kindled a fresh desire;
Then did she lift her hand unto his breast,
A part as white and youthful as the rest,
Where, as his flowery breath still comes and goes,
She felt his gentle heart pant through his clothes.

At last she took her hand from off that part,
And said it panted like another's heart: 800
'Why should it be more feeble and less bold?
Why should the blood about it be more cold?
Nay, sure, that yields, only thy tongue denies,
And the true fancy of thy heart belies.'
Then did she lift her hand unto his chin,
And prais'd the pretty dimpling of his skin:
But straight his chin she 'gan to overslip,
When she beheld the redness of his lip,
And said, 'Thy lips are soft; press them to mine,
And thou shalt see they are as soft as thine.'   810
Then would she fain have gone unto his eye,
But still his ruddy lip, standing so nigh,
Drew her hand back, therefore his eye she miss'd,
'Ginning to clasp his neck, and would have kiss'd.
But then the boy did struggle to be gone,
Vowing to leave her and that place alone:
But then bright Salmacis began to fear,
And said, 'Fair stranger, I will leave thee here,
Amid these pleasant places, all alone.'
So turning back, she feignèd to be gone: 820
But from his sight she had no power to pass,
Therefore she turn'd and hid her in the grass;
When to the ground bending her snow-white knee,
The glad earth gave new coats to every tree.
    He then, supposing he was all alone,
Like a young boy that is espied of none,
Runs here and there; then on the banks doth look,
Then on the crystal current of the brook;
Then with his feet he touch'd the silver streams,
Whose drowsy waves made music in their dreams,   830
And, for he was not wholly in, did weep,
Talking aloud and babbling in their sleep;
Whose pleasant coolness when the boy did feel,
He thrust his foot down lower to the heel;
O'ercome with whose sweet noise, he did begin
To strip his soft clothes from his tender skin.
When straight the scorching Sun wept tears of brine,
Because he durst not touch him with his shine,
For fear of spoiling that same ivory skin

Whose whiteness he so much delighted in;   840
And then the Moon, mother of mortal ease,
Would fain have come from the Antipodes
To have beheld him naked as he stood,
Ready to leap into the silver flood;
But might not: for the laws of Heaven deny
To shew men's secrets to a woman's eye;
And therefore was her sad and gloomy light
Confin'd unto the secret-keeping night.
    When beauteous Salmacis a while had gaz'd
Upon his naked corpse, she stood amaz'd,   850
And both her sparkling eyes burnt in her face,
Like the bright sun reflected in a glass:
Scarce can she stay from running to the boy,
Scarce can she now defer her hopèd joy;
So fast her youthful blood plays in her veins,
That, almost mad, she scarce herself contains;
When young Hermaphroditus, as he stands
Clapping his white sides with his hollow hands,
Leapt lively from the land whereon he stood
Into the main part of the crystal flood: 860
Like ivory then his snowy body was,
Or a white lily in a crystal glass.
The rose the water-nymph from where she lay,
As having won the glory of the day,
And her light garments cast from off her skin;
'He's mine,' she cried, and so leapt sprightly in.
The flattering ivy who did ever see
Inclasp the huge trunk of an agèd tree,
Let him behold the young boy as he stands
Inclasp'd in wanton Salmacis' hands.   870
Betwixt those ivory arms she lock'd him fast,
Striving to get away; till at the last,
Fondling she said, 'Why striv'st thou to be gone?
Why shouldst thou so desire to be alone?
Thy cheek is never fair when none is by;
For what is red and white but to the eye?
And for that cause the heavens are dark at night,
Because all creatures close their weary sight;
For there's no mortal can so early rise
But still the morning waits upon his eyes.   880

The early-rising and soon-singing lark
Can never chant her sweet notes in the dark;
For sleep she ne'er so little or so long,
Yet still the morning will attend her song.
All creatures that beneath bright Cynthia be
Have appetite unto society:
The overflowing waves would have a bound
Within the confines of the spacious ground,
And all their shady currents would be plac'd
In hollow of the solitary vast,   890
But that they loathe to let their soft streams sing
Where none can hear their gentle murmuring.'
Yet still the boy, regardless what she said,
Struggled apace to overswim the maid;
Which when the nymph perceiv'd, she 'gan to say,
'Struggle thou mayst, but never get away:
So grant, just gods, that never day may see
The separation 'twixt this boy and me!'
    The gods did hear her prayer, and feel her woe;
And in one body they began to grow: 900
She felt his youthful blood in every vein,
And he felt hers warm his cold breast again;
And ever since was woman's love so blest,
That it will draw blood from the strongest breast.
Nor man nor maid now could they be esteem'd,
Neither, and either, might they well be deem'd:
When the young boy, Hermaphroditus, said,
With the set voice of neither man nor maid,
'Swift Mercury, thou author of my life,
And thou my mother, Vulcan's lovely wife,   910
Let your poor offspring's latest breath be blest
In but obtaining this his last request;
Grant that whoe'er, heated by Phoebus' beams,
Shall come to cool him in these silver streams,
May never more a manly shape retain,
But half a virgin may return again!'
His parents hearken'd to his last request,
And with that great power they the fountain blest;
And since that time who in that fountain swims,
A maiden smoothness seizeth half his limbs.   920

John Marston

The Metamorphosis of Pygmalion's Image
(1598)

Pygmalion, whose chaste mind all the beauties in Cyprus could not ensnare, yet at the length having carved in ivory an excellent proportion of a beauteous woman, was so deeply enamoured on his own workmanship, that he would oftentimes lay the image in bed with him, and fondly use such petitions and dalliance, as if it had been a breathing creature. But in the end, finding his fond dotage, and yet persevering in his ardent affection, made his devout prayers to Venus, that she would vouchsafe to inspire life into his love, and then join them both together in marriage. Whereupon Venus graciously condescending to his earnest suit, the maid (by the power of her deity), was metamorphosed into a living woman. And after, Pygmalion (being in Cyprus) begat a son of her, which was called Paphus, whereupon that island Cyprus, in honour of Venus, was after, and is now, called by the inhabitants, Paphos.

1

Pygmalion, whose high love-hating mind
Disdain'd to yield servile affection
Or amorous suit to any womankind,
Knowing their wants, and men's perfection:
   Yet love at length forc'd him to know his fate,
   And love the shade whose substance he did hate.

2

For having wrought in purest ivory
So fair an image of a woman's feature,
That never yet proudest mortality
Could show so rare and beauteous a creature 10
   (Unless my mistress' all-excelling face,
   Which gives to beauty beauty's only grace).

3

He was amaz'd at the wondrous rareness
Of his own workmanship's perfection.
He thought that Nature ne'er produc'd such fairness
In which all beauties have their mansion;
    And thus admiring, was enamoured
    On that fair image himself portrayed.

4

And naked as it stood before his eyes,
Imperious Love declares his deity.   20
O, what alluring beauties he descries
In each part of his fair imagery!
    Her nakedness each beauteous shape contains,
    All beauty in her nakedness remains.

5

He thought he saw the blood run through the vein,
And leap and swell with all alluring means:
Then fears he is deceiv'd, and then again
He thinks he sees the brightness of the beams
    Which shoot from out the fairness of her eye:
    At which he stands as in an ecstasy.   30

6

Her amber-coloured, her shining hair,
Makes him protest, the sun hath spread her head
With golden beams, to make her far more fair.
But when her cheeks his amorous thoughts have fed,
    Then he exclaims 'Such red and so pure white,
    Did never bless the eye of mortal sight.'

7

Then views her lips – no lips did seem so fair
In his conceit – through which he thinks doth fly
So sweet a breath that doth perfume the air.
Then next her dimpl'd chin he doth descry,   40
    And views, and wonders, and yet views her still.
    Love's eyes in viewing never have their fill.

8

Her breasts like polish'd ivory appear,
Whose modest mount do bless admiring eye,
And makes him wish for such a pillowbeer.
Thus fond Pygmalion striveth to descry
  Each beauteous part, not letting overslip
  One parcel of his curious workmanship:

9

Until his eye descended so far down
That it descried love's pavilion: 50
Where Cupid doth enjoy his only crown,
And Venus hath her chiefest mansion:
  There would he wink, and winking look again;
  Both eyes and thoughts would gladly there remain.

10

Whoever saw the subtile City-dame
In sacred church, when her pure thoughts should pray,
Peer through her fingers, so to hide her shame,
When that her eye her mind would fain bewray:
  So would he view, and wink, and view again,
  A chaster thought could not his eyes retain.   60

11

He wonder'd that she blush'd not when his eye
Saluted those same parts of secrecy:
Conceiting not it was imagery
That kindly yielded that large liberty.
  (O that my mistress were an image too,
  That I might blameless her perfections view.)

12

But when the fair proportion of her thigh
Began appear: 'O, Ovid,' would he cry,
'Did e'er Corinna show such ivory
When she appear'd in Venus' livery?'   70
  And thus enamour'd, dotes on his own art,
  Which he did work to work his pleasing smart.

13

And fondly doting, oft he kiss'd her lip.
Oft would he dally with her ivory breasts.
No wanton love-trick would he overslip,
But still observ'd all amorous behests
    Whereby he thought he might procure the love
    Of his dull image, which no plaints could move.

14

Look how the peevish Papists crouch, and kneel
To some dumb idol with their offering,   80
As if a senseless carved stone could feel
The ardour of his bootless chattering,
    So fond he was, and earnest in his suit,
    To his remorseless image, dumb and mute.

15

He oft doth wish his soul might part in sunder,
So that one half in her had residence:
Oft he exclaims, 'O, beauty's only wonder,
Sweet model of delight, fair excellence,
    Be gracious unto him that formed thee,
    Compassionate his true love's ardency.'   90

16

She with her silence seems to grant his suit.
Then he all jocund, like a wanton lover,
With amorous embracements doth salute
Her slender waist, presuming to discover
    The vale of love, where Cupid doth delight
    To sport, and dally all the sable night.

17

His eyes, her eyes, kindly encounter'd,
His breast, her breast, oft joined close unto,
His arms' embracements oft she suffer'd,
Hands, arms, eyes, tongue, lips, and all parts did woo.   100
    His thigh with hers, his knee play'd with her knee,
    A happy consort when all parts agree.

18

But when he saw, poor soul, he was deceiv'd,
(Yet scarce he could believe his sense had fail'd)
Yet when he found all hope from him bereav'd,
And saw how fondly all his thoughts had err'd,
   Then did he like to poor Ixion seem,
   That clipp'd a cloud instead of heaven's queen.

19

I oft have smil'd to see the foolery
Of some sweet youths, who seriously protest   110
That love respects not actual luxury,
But only joys to dally, sport and jest:
   Love is a child, contented with a toy;
   A busk-point or some favour stills the boy.

20

Mark my Pygmalion, whose affection's ardour
May be a mirror to posterity.
Yet viewing, touching, kissing (common favour)
Could never satiate his love's ardency:
   And therefore, ladies, think that they ne'er love you
   Who do not unto more than kissing move you.   120

21

For my Pygmalion, kiss'd, view'd and embrac'd,
And yet exclaims, 'Why were these women made,
O sacred gods, and with such beauties grac'd?
Have they not power as well to cool and shade
   As for to heat men's hearts? or is there none,
   Or are they all, like mine, relentless stone?'

22

With that he takes her in his loving arms,
And down within a down-bed softly laid her.
Then on his knees he all his senses charms,
To invocate sweet Venus for to raise her   130
   To wished life, and to infuse some breath
   To that which, dead, yet gave a life to death.

23

'Thou sacred queen of sportive dallying,'
(Thus he begins), 'Love's only emperess,
Whose kingdom rests in wanton revelling,
Let me beseech thee show thy powerfulness
   In changing stone to flesh! make her relent,
   And kindly yield to thy sweet blandishment!

24

'O, gracious gods, take compassion!
Instil into her some celestial fire,   140
That she may equalize affection,
And have a mutual love, and love's desire.
   Thou know'st the force of love! then pity me,
   Compassionate my true love's ardency.'

25

Thus having said, he riseth from the floor,
As if his soul divin'd him good fortune,
Hoping his prayers to pity mov'd some power,
For all his thoughts did all good luck importune.
   And therefore straight he strips him naked quite,
   That in the bed he might have more delight.   150

26

'Then thus, sweet sheets,' he says, 'which now do cover
The idol of my soul, the fairest one
That ever lov'd, or had an amorous lover,
Earth's only model of perfection:
   Sweet happy sheets, deign for to take me in,
   That I my hopes and longing thoughts may win.'

27

With that his nimble limbs do kiss the sheets,
And now he bows him for to lay him down,
And now each part with her fair parts do meet,
Now doth he hope for to enjoy love's crown: 160
   Now do they dally, kiss, embrace together,
   Like Leda's twins at sight of fairer weather.

28

Yet all's conceit, but shadow of that bliss
Which now my muse strives sweetly to display
In this my wondrous metamorphosis.
Deign to believe me, now I sadly say:
   The stony substance of his image feature
   Was straight transform'd into a living creature.

29

For when his hands her fair-form'd limbs had felt,
And that his arms her naked waist embrac'd,   170
Each part like wax before the sun did melt;
And now, oh now, he finds how he is grac'd
   By his own work. Tut, women will relent
   When as they find such moving blandishment.

30

Do but conceive a mother's passing gladness,
(After that death her only son hath seiz'd
And overwhelm'd her soul with endless sadness)
When that she sees him gin for to be rais'd
   From out his deadly swoon to life again:
   Such joy Pygmalion feels in every vein.   180

31

And yet he fears he doth but dreaming find
So rich content and such celestial bliss.
Yet when he proves and finds her wondrous kind,
Yielding soft touch for touch, sweet kiss for kiss,
   He's well assur'd no fair imagery
   Could yield such pleasing, love's felicity.

32

O, wonder not to hear me thus relate,
And say to flesh transformed was a stone.
Had I my love in such a wished state
As was afforded to Pygmalion,   190
   Though flinty hard, of her you soon should see
   As strange a transformation wrought by me.

33

And now methinks some wanton itching ear
With lustful thoughts and ill attention,
Lists to my muse, expecting for to hear
The amorous description of that action
    Which Venus seeks, and ever doth require,
    When fitness grants a place to please desire.

34

Let him conceit but what himself would do
When that he had obtained such a favour   200
Of her to whom his thoughts were bound unto,
If she, in recompense of his love's labour,
    Would deign to let one pair of sheets contain
    The willing bodies of those loving twain.

35

Could he, oh, could he, when that each to either
Did yield kind kissing, and more kind embracing,
Could he when that they felt, and clipp'd together,
And might enjoy the life of dallying,
    Could he abstain midst such a wanton sporting
    From doing that which is not fit reporting?   210

36

What would he do when that her softest skin
Saluted his with a delightful kiss?
When all things fit for love's sweet pleasuring
Invited him to reap a lover's bliss?
    What he would do, the self-same action
    Was not neglected by Pygmalion.

37

For when he found that life had took his seat
Within the breast of his kind beauteous love,
When that he found that warmth and wished heat
Which might a saint and coldest spirit move,   220
    Then arms, eyes, hands, tongue, lips and wanton thigh
    Were willing agents in love's luxury.

38

Who knows not what ensues? O, pardon me,
Ye gaping ears that swallow up my lines:
Expect no more. Peace, idle poesy,
Be not obscene, though wanton in thy rhymes;
   And chaster thoughts, pardon if I do trip,
   Or if some loose lines from my pen do slip.

39

Let this suffice, that that same happy night
So gracious were the gods of marriage,   230
Mid'st all their pleasing and long-wish'd delight
Paphus was got: of whom in after-age
   Cyprus was Paphos call'd, and evermore
   Those islanders do Venus' name adore.

NOTES

———

p. xxix Petrarchanism: literary concept of love associated with the sonnets of the Italian poet Petrarch (1304–74) and his manner of expression.

p. xxxiv anaphora: repetition of the same word or phrase at the beginning of several successive clauses or lines of verse.

p. xxxiv paradox: phrase or statement apparently self-contradictory in form.

p. xxxiv chiasmus: inversion in a second phrase or clause of the word order in the first.

p. xxxiv feminine rhyme: rhyme where the final syllable is unstressed.

p. xxxiv dactyls: metrical foot consisting of one long (or stressed) syllable followed by two short (or unstressed).

p. xl masculine rhyme: rhyme where the final syllable is stressed.

p. 4 thou canst talk by proof of wavering pelf: you can argue from the experience of uncertain fortune.

p. 5 the Delian harper: Apollo, who was born on the island of Delos.

p. 6 the Theban: Hercules, who was born at Thebes.

p. 7 the sweet Arcadian boy: Adonis.

p. 8 Latmian love: Endymion.

p. 9 Pallas' flower: possibly the olive, sacred to Pallas, although it is not a flower or pale.

p. 10 moly: herb with magical properties given by Hermes to Ulysses on Circe's island.

p. 10 Ajax blossom: the hyacinth, which sprang from Ajax's blood when he killed himself after an unsuccessful contest with Ulysses for the arms of Achilles.

p. 11 Nereus: old man of the sea, with magical ability to change his shape; father of the Nereids, sea-nymphs.

p. 11 With pebbles stop their beaks to make them mute: the geese take pebbles into their beaks so that their cackling will not betray them to the eagles.

p. 12 Hybla: town in Sicily renowned for the quality of its honey.

p. 19 Queen of Sea: Thetis.

p. 19 Paphian Queen of Love: Venus, who came to Cyprus (Paphos) when she was born.

p. 20 her lovely son: Cupid.

p. 24 fatal bird of augury: either the owl or the raven, both of which are birds of ill omen in Pliny.

p. 28 Alonely: variant of 'alone'.

p. 40 caparisons: archaic term for horse's trappings, bridle, saddle, etc.

p. 54 Wat: type-name for a hare.

p. 71 Hellespont: gulf at the Western end of the Sea of Marmora, separating Turkey in Europe from Turkey in Asia Minor.

p. 73 [he] That leapt into the water for a kiss/Of his own shadow, and despising many,/Died ere he could enjoy the love of any: Narcissus.

p. 73 sea-nymphs' inveigling harmony: the song of the Sirens, which lured sailors to destruction.

p. 74 Idalian Ganymede: Ganymede, Jove's lover, connected with Mount Ida.

p. 82 Midas' brood: wealthy people, by association with rich King Midas.

p. 84 Aesop's cock: reference to a fable by Aesop (*c.* 570 BC) in which a cock finds a rare jewel where he would have preferred to find a grain of corn.

p. 85 ribband: ribbon.

p. 86 that sapphire-visag'd god: Neptune.

p. 93 prodromus: forerunner.

p. 93 the queen of love: Venus.

p. 95 the god of love: Cupid.

p. 96 deceive her in a shower of gold: *see* Danae

p. 96 like a swan, come to her naked bed: as Jove did to seduce Leda.

p. 100 Etna: volcanic mountain in Sicily.

p. 100 collogues that night: coaxes or flatters during that night.

p. 102 look: look at.

p. 104 catchpoles: sheriff's officers who arrest for debt.

p. 107 Alcmena: alternative form of Alcmene.

p. 109 the little god: Cupid

p. 110 that boy/That scorned to let a beauteous nymph enjoy ... needs would love himself: Narcissus.

p. 112 th'Arcadian lass: Diana.

GLOSSARY OF NAMES

ABYDOS, a town on the Hellespont, in Asia Minor, opposite *Sestos*

ACHERON, one of the rivers of Hades

ACHILLES, son of Peleus and *Thetis*; in infancy he was bathed in the river *Styx* to render him immortal, but the heel by which his mother held him remained untouched and vulnerable. The greatest of the Greek heroes in the Trojan war, he was killed by Paris. According to the Delphic oracle, only filings from Achilles' spear could heal the wounds it made

ACTAEON a huntsman who was changed into a stag and killed by his own hounds as a punishment for seeing *Diana* and her *Nymphs* naked while bathing

ADONIS, a youth loved by *Venus*; he was fatally wounded by a wild boar. Anemones sprang up where his blood spilled on the ground

ALCIDES, *Hercules*

ALCMENE seduced by *Jupiter*, who assumed the form of her husband, and caused the wedding night to last three days

AMARANTH, a flower which would never fade

AMBROSIA, the food of the gods, which made all who partook of it immortal

AMYNTAS, a shepherd boy loved by *Venus*; or a shepherd from Virgil's Eclogues, hero of Tasso's *Aminta* (1573)

ANGELICA, character in Boiardo's *Orlando Innamorato* (1488), continued in Ariosto's *Orlando Furioso* (1552); daughter of the King of Cathay, she was loved by Orlando (*Roland*), but herself loved, and married, Medoro (*Medor*)

APOLLO, god of the sun, god of music and poetry

ARGUS, a many-eyed monster, who guarded Io from the attentions of *Jupiter*, but was killed by *Mercury*

ARIADNE, daughter of Minos and Pasiphae; she fell in love with Theseus and helped him kill the Minotaur and then escape from the Labyrinth, but he abandoned her on Naxos. Dionysus subsequently married her, and gave her a diadem made by Hephaestus, which became a constellation

ASTRAEA, daughter of *Jupiter*; the personification of justice and virtue, she abandoned the earth because of its wickedness

ATE, goddess of discord, the personification of delusion

ATLAS, a Giant, grandfather of *Mercury*; after the revolt of the *Giants*, he was sentenced by Jupiter to carry the vault of the sky on his shoulders

AURORA, the personification of dawn.

BACCHUS, god of wine, son of *Jupiter*.

CARIA, region of Asia Minor, adjoining *Lycia*.

CÄYSTER, a river of Asia, near Ephesus, famous for its swans

CEPHALUS, seduced by *Aurora*, he later abandoned her

CHAOS, oldest of the gods; the embodiment of the primeval void

CHELIS, a sea *Nymph*, or Nereid

CIRCE, an enchantress who transformed Ulysses' companions into animals

CLORE, a sea *Nymph*, or Nereid

COCYTUS, one of the rivers of Hades

COLCHIS, a town on the Black Sea, from whence Jason recovered the Golden Fleece

CORINNA, Ovid's mistress in the *Amores*

CUPID, son of *Venus*, the personification of love

CYCLOPES, a race of one-eyed Giants, assistants to *Vulcan*

CYNTHIA, *Diana*, the moon goddess

CYTHERA, an island in the Peloponnese, associated with *Venus*

DANAE, princess of Argos; she was confined to a tower by her father, but seduced by *Jupiter*, who took the form of a shower of gold

DESTINIES, the Parcae, or Fates; three goddesses depicted as spinning thread which determined the span of mortal lives

DIANA, goddess of the hunt; the personification of virginity; goddess of the moon

DIS, Pluto, king of the underworld

ECHO, a *Nymph* of the trees and springs; her love for *Narcissus* was unrequited, and she pined away, leaving only her voice

ELYSIUM, part of the underworld where the inhabitants enjoyed eternal bliss

ENDYMION, a young shepherd, endowed with the gift of eternal sleep, and hence eternal youth; he was loved by *Diana*

EOS, *Aurora*

ERYCINA, *Venus*

EUROPA, a Phoenician princess; she was seduced by *Jupiter* in the form of a bull

EUROTA, the chief river of Laconia, the site of Sparta

FAUNS, field or harvest spirits, identified with the *Satyrs*

GANYMEDE, youthful male lover and cup-bearer to *Jupiter*

GIANTS, the children of Gaia, the earth; they revolted against the gods but were defeated

GLAUCUS, a fisherman who ate of a herb which made him immortal; the sea goddesses cleansed him of mortality, and as a sea god he was endowed with the gift of prophecy; he courted *Scylla* and *Ariadne*, both unsuccessfully

GRACES, personifications of grace and beauty

HARPIES, winged female demons, who carried off souls

HEBE, daughter and cup-bearer (until replaced by *Ganymede*) to *Jupiter*

HELLE, daughter of Athamas, king of Thebes; she fled from her stepmother on a flying ram, but fell into the sea and drowned in the spot known as the Hellespont

HERCULES, son of *Jupiter*; he was famed for his strength, which enabled him to perform twelve heroic labours at the behest of his cousin Eurystheus

HERMAPHRODITUS, son of *Hermes* and Aphrodite (*Venus*); he was loved by *Salmacis*, a *Nymph*, whose advances he rejected; when he bathed in her lake she became united with him in a single body

HERMES, *Mercury*

HERPERIDES, *Nymphs* of the setting sun, guardians of the Golden Apples, the search for which was one of the labours of *Hercules*

HESPERUS, the evening star

HIPPOLYTUS, son of Theseus; his stepmother Phaedra fell in love with him, and when he rejected her, she accused him of rape. As a result, his father sought vengeance, and Hippolytus was killed when his horses were frightened by *Neptune*

HYMEN, god of marriage

IDA (IDE), a mountain near Troy

IDALIUM, a town in Cyprus with a grove sacred to *Venus*

ISIS, the River Thames at Oxford, where Lodge studied

IXION, he tried to seduce Juno, wife of *Jupiter*, but instead he coupled with a cloud made in her shape by her husband, giving rise to the race of Centaurs, which were half man and half horse, hence 'Ixion's shaggy-footed race' (*HL*, I, 114)

JOVE, *Jupiter*

JUPITER, king of the gods; he was the husband of Juno, but had many love affairs, often transforming himself into different shapes in order to carry out his seductions

LATMUS, mountain in *Caria*

LEDA, mother of Clytemnestra, Helen, and the twins, or Dioscuri – Castor and Pollux; she coupled with Jupiter who took the form of a swan to seduce her

LEUCOTHOE, lover of Helios, the sun, who was equated with Apollo

LUCINA, goddess of childbirth, identified with *Diana*, the moon goddess, or Juno, wife of *Jupiter*

LYCIA, coastal region of Asia Minor, adjoining *Caria*

MARS, god of war, lover of *Venus*

MEANDER, a river in Phrygia, noted for its winding course

MEDOR, see *Angelica*

MERCURY, son of *Jupiter*, messenger of the gods, inventor of the lyre, patron of thieves; his attributes included the caduceus, or wand, and a broad-brimmed hat

MIDAS, mythical king of Phrygia; everything he touched turned to gold

MOLY, a herb possessing magical powers

MORPHEUS, god of sleep and dreams

MUSAEUS, fifth-century Greek author of a poem on Hero and Leander

MUSES, nine daughters of *Jupiter*, presiding over the arts

NECTAR, the drink of the gods, which made all who partook of it immortal

NAIS, a sea *Nymph*, or Nereid

NARCISSUS, a handsome youth who, though beloved by many, loved none, until he fell in love with his own reflection in a pool, where he stayed watching it until he died

NEPTUNE, god of the sea

NYMPHS, goddesses or spirits of the fields or of nature in general

OLYMPUS, a mountain on the border of Macedonia and Thessaly, which was the abode of the gods

OPS, wife of *Saturn* and mother of *Jupiter*

OSSA, a mountain in Thessaly

PALEMON, son of Ino, turned into a sea-god by *Neptune* when Ino leapt into the sea with him to save him from the mad wrath of his father Athamas

PALLAS, virgin goddess of war, philosophy, the arts, and domestic pursuits; often known as Pallas Athene

PAPHOS, daughter of Pygmalion and the statue; the island of Cyprus was called Paphos in her honour

PELION, a mountain in Thessaly, piled on top of *Ossa* by the *Giants* in their attempt to storm heaven

PELOPS, son of *Tantalus*; he was killed by his father and served up at a feast for the gods; only his shoulder was consumed, and it was subsequently replaced with one of ivory

PHAETHON, son of *Apollo*; he tried to drive the chariot of the sun, but lost control and was destroyed when he came too near to the earth.

PHOEBUS, *Apollo*

PROMETHEUS, he stole fire from the gods and gave it to mortals, for which he was bound to a rock where an eagle continually devoured his liver

PROTEUS, a sea god; he was able to change his shape at will

PYGMALION, king of Cyprus, he fell in love with a statue, and asked *Venus* to grant him a woman resembling it, whereupon it came to life; they then married and had a daughter called *Paphos*

PYTHON, a dragon with the gift of prophecy, perceived by Apollo as a rival and killed by him

ROLAND, see *Angelica*

SALMACIS, a *Nymph* who loved Hermaphroditus, with whom she became united in a single body

SATURN, father of *Jupiter*, dethroned by his son

SATYR, a demon of nature; part goat, part man

SCYLLA, beloved of *Glaucus*, who scorned the love of *Circe* on her account; in consequence, Circe transformed her into a monster in the form of a woman with six dogs' heads around the lower part of her body. This monster lived in the straits of Messina, and the creatures devoured all who came within their reach

SESTOS, a town on the Thracian side of the Hellespont, opposite *Abydos*

SIBYLLA, the wise Sybil, a prophetess

SILENUS, an old *Satyr*

SILVANUS, a god of the woods, lover of a youth (Cyparissus) who was turned into a cypress tree

SISYPHUS, the most cunning of mortals, and founder of Corinth; he was condemned continually to roll a rock up a mountain in the underworld

STYX, one of the rivers of Hades

TANTALUS, son of Jupiter; he served up his son *Pelops* at a feast for the gods. He was condemned to continual hunger and thirst near water which receded when he tried to drink, and trees with fruit which sprang out of reach when he tried to eat

TAURUS, a mountain range, stretching from the Euphrates to the Aegean Sea

THEMIS, a sea *Nymph*, or Nereid

THETIS, the most important of the sea goddesses known as Nereids

TITAN, the sun

TRITON, a sea god, son of *Neptune*, depicted as blowing into a shell used as a horn

VENUS, goddess of love; wife of *Vulcan*, she was the lover of Mars, and had other love affairs

VESTALS, virgin priestesses who tended the sacred fire in the temple of Vesta, the goddess of the domestic hearth

VULCAN, the lame god of fire, husband of *Venus*, blacksmith of the gods

ZEPHYRUS, god of the east wind

SUGGESTIONS FOR FURTHER READING

Alexander, Nigel, ed., *Elizabethan Narrative Verse* (London: Edward Arnold, 1967). Contains, in addition to the poems of Lodge, Marlowe and Beaumont, narrative poems by Chapman, Daniel, Drayton, and Fletcher, with a critical introduction and notes.

Bradbrook, Muriel, *Shakespeare and Elizabethan Poetry* (Cambridge: Cambridge University Press, 1951). Has stimulating chapter on the flood of Ovidian verse in the 1590s.

Bush, Douglas, *Mythology and the Renaissance Tradition in English Poetry* (New York: Norton, 1932, rev.ed., 1963). Learned and wide-ranging survey of the influence of Classical literature on Renaissance poetry, with chapters on Ovid and the major Ovidian poems. Critical attitudes interestingly dated.

Donno, Elizabeth Story, ed., *Elizabethan Minor Epics* (London: Routledge, 1963). Contains a somewhat different selection of poems from Alexander (see above), including Heywood, Edwards and Weever; excellent critical introduction. See also her useful article 'The epyllion' in *English Poetry and Phrase 1540–1674*, ed., Christopher Ricks, Sphere History of Literature in the English Language (London: Sphere Books, 1970).

Duncan-Jones, Katherine, 'Much Ado with Red and White: The Earliest Readers of Shakespeare's *Venus and Adonis*', *Review of English Studies* XLIV (1993), pp. 479–501. Informative and amusing article on the early reception of Shakespeare's poem.

Hulse, Clark, *Metamorphic Verse: The Elizabethan Minor Epic* (Princeton: Princeton University Press, 1981). Detailed and informative on Ovidian poetry in the context of the Elizabethan literary system.

Keach, William, *Elizabethan Erotic Narratives* (New Brunswick, New Jersey: Rutgers University Press, 1977). Covers similar ground to Hulse, but particularly good on Ovid.

Lanham, Richard, *The Motives of Eloquence* (New Haven and London: Yale University Press, 1976). Lively and readable chapters on Shakespeare and Ovid in the context of a study of Renaissance attitudes to rhetoric.

Lewis, C. S. *English Literature in the Sixteenth Century, excluding Drama* (Oxford: Clarendon Press, 1954). Now much disputed, but still provocative accounts of the major Ovidian poems.

Miller, Paul W. 'The Elizabethan Minor Epic', *Studies in Philology* LV (1958), pp. 31–8. Discusses the relation of Elizabethan Ovidian poems to the category of Alexandrian Greek poems known as epyllia. See also Walter Allen Jr, 'The Non-Existent Classical Epyllion', *Studies in Philology* LV (1958), pp. 575–8, which challenges Miller's views.

Miller, R. P. 'The Myth of Mars' Hot Minion' in *Venus and Adonis*, *English Literary History* XXVI (1959). Reads the poems as a comment on 'Petrarchan norms' of behaviour, and on the irrationality of passion. See also Miller's 'Venus, Adonis, and the Horses', *English Literary History* XIX (1952).

Otis, Brooks, *Ovid as an Epic Poet* (Cambridge: Cambridge University Press, 1966). Useful study of the *Metamorphoses*, stressing Ovid's ideal of 'mutual, conjugal, heterosexual love'.

Reese, M. M. ed., *Elizabethan Verse Romances* (London: Routledge and Kegan Paul, 1968). Includes poems by Lodge, Marlowe, Shakespeare, Daniel, Drayton, and Marston, with introduction and notes.

Smith, Bruce R., *Homosexual Desire in Shakespeare's England: A Cultural Poetics* (Chicago and London: Chicago University Press, 1991). Provocative reading of Marlowe and Beaumont in the context of homoerotic writing of the period.

Smith, Hallett, *Elizabethan Poetry: A Study in Conventions, Meaning and Expression* (Ann Arbor: University of Michigan Press, 1968). Standard account of Ovidian poetry in a wide survey of Elizabethan poetic genres.

Steane, J. B., *Marlowe, A Critical Study* (Cambridge: Cambridge University Press, 1964). Sensitive chapter on Marlowe's handling of emotion in *Hero and Leander*.

Thompson, Ann, 'Death by Water: The Originality of *Salmacis and Hermaphroditus*', *Modern Language Quarterly* 40 (1979), pp. 99–114. Argues that the poem takes a negative view of bisexuality.

Turner, Myron, 'Pastoral and Hermaphrodite: A Study in the Naturalism of Marlowe's *Hero and Leander*', *Texas Studies in Literature and Language* 17 (1975) 397–444. In contrast to Smith (see above), sees the poem's 'erotic anarchy' as evidence of a 'desire for order'.

Watson, Donald G., 'The Contrarieties of *Venus and Adonis*', *Studies in Philology* 75 (1978), 32–63. Includes useful survey of the variety of different readings of the poem.

Weiss, Adam, 'Rhetoric and Satire: New Light on John Marston's The *Metamorphosis of Pygmalian's Image and the Satires*', *Journal of English and Germanic Philology* LXXI (1972), 22–35. Argues for a reading of Marston's poem as a satirical comment on the Ovidian genre.

Wilkinson, L. P. *Ovid Recalled* (Cambridge: Cambridge University Press, 1955). The most useful background book on Ovid, with a chapter on his influence on English Renaissance literature.

Scylla's Metamorphosis

The narrator encounters the sorrowful Glaucus by the River Thames (1–48). Nymphs assemble, but Glaucus bids them leave him to his sorrow (49–198). The nymphs attempt to comfort him, and eventually he tells them the cause of his woe (199–228). He fell in love with Scylla and tried to woo her, but she rejected him (229–372). Banished from her, he went abroad and took up residence by the River Thames (373–420). The nymphs weep to hear him, and led by Thetis they pray to Venus to assist Glaucus (421–98). Venus and Cupid appear, and a dart from Cupid's bow cures Glaucus of his love (499–564). Scylla then arrives on the river, and Cupid shoots a dart at her which makes her fall in love with Glaucus (565–600). She tries to woo him, but he is disdainful, and she departs for Sicily in despair (601–60). All follow and see Scylla transformed into a rocky isle, which all creatures shun (661–750). The other characters feast in Neptune's palace before retiring to rest, and the narrator is urged by Glaucus to let the world know of Scylla's pride (751–86).

Venus and Adonis

Adonis starts out to hunt at dawn, when Venus begins to woo him and pulls him from his horse, but he is reluctant, and she entreats him until midday (1–180). He continues to resist and she continues to entice him, comparing her body to a deer park (181–240). He breaks away and goes to mount his horse, but it spies a female horse with which it gallops away (241–324). Adonis sits down cursing, and Venus steals up to him, and urges him to follow the example of his horse (325–408). Adonis replies that the only love he knows is the hunt, but Venus compares him to a banquet (409–50). When he is about to speak again she falls down in anticipation of what he is going to say, and believing she is dead, he tries to revive her, and kisses her, and she longs for more kisses (451–522). Adonis pleads that he is young and that evening has come, but he agrees to kiss her goodnight. She kisses him, and they fall to the ground and embrace until, out of pity, she agrees to let him go (523–82). She asks if they can meet the following day, but he says he intends to hunt the boar. She pulls him to the ground on top of her, but he will do no more (583–612). She then tries to dissuade him from his intention to hunt, with fearful images of the boar and a prophecy of his death. She also tries to persuade him to hunt the hare instead (613–714). He urges her to leave because night is coming on, but she urges him to make the most of his uncertain mortality, and he ends by accusing her of lust (715–810). Adonis leaves Venus to lament (811–52). Dawn breaks and Venus hears Adonis' hounds, and then spies the boar and wounded hounds (853–924). Venus rails against death, and is overcome with tears until she hears a huntsman's call, which she takes for Adonis, and her spirits revive (925–1026). Then she finds Adonis dead from a wound inflicted by the boar, and laments through her tears (1027–1136). Venus prophesies that, Adonis being dead, love shall henceforth be unhappy (1137–64). Adonis's body melts away, and from his blood on the ground a purple flower springs up, which Venus plucks and places in her breast before she hurries away to Paphos, intending to immure herself (1165–94).

Hero and Leander

I: the beautiful Hero lives at Sestos, and the handsome Leander at Abydos, on opposite sides of the Hellespont (1–90). They meet at an annual feast in the Temple of Venus, which is decorated with erotic images, and they fall in love at first sight (91–166). Leander woos Hero, arguing at length against virginity (167–330). Hero's looks show that he has won her, but she feigns anger (331–40). Leander tries to embrace her, and she recoils, but she invites him to her tower, far from the town. Although she tries to resist her own inclinations, Cupid shoots a dart at her (341–376). Cupid then flies to the palace of the Destinies to entreat them to allow Hero and Leander to enjoy one another, but the Destinies will not agree, for the hate they bear towards Cupid (377–85). This is because once Mercury tried to seduce a country maid by giving her a draught of nectar, for which Jupiter expelled him from heaven. Cupid undertook to help Mercury gain revenge by causing the Destinies to fall in love with him (386–450). Mercury then requested of them that they cause Jupiter to be deposed, but when this was accomplished Mercury forsook the Destinies, who in consequence turned against both him and Cupid, and restored Jupiter (451–64). Mercury returned to heaven, but to avenge themselves the Destinies decreed that learning shall always be held in low esteem (465–84).
II: Hero leaves Leander, but they send letters, and then Leander comes to her tower by night, and they embrace (1–32). However, Leander is innocent, and Hero coy, and their love is not consummated (37–86). Dawn begins to break and they part, but Leander's demeanour reveals that he is in love, and he finally strips and dives into the Hellespont to

swim back to her tower (87–154). Neptune tries to seduce him, but Leander is deaf to his entreaties, and eventually reaches Hero's tower (155–226). The sight of a naked man at her door affrights her, and she seeks refuge in bed (227–44). Leander comes into the bed, if only for warmth, and although Hero at first resists him, their love is consummated (245–306). She tries to rise and leave him, but he catches her and sees her naked, just as dawn breaks (307–34).

Salmacis and Hermaphroditus

Invocation to Venus (1–12). A lovely boy, son of Mercury and Venus and therefore named Hermaphroditus, beloved of the gods and nymphs, travels abroad and comes to a brook (13–102). Here the nymph Salmacis dwells, and is courted by Jupiter, but she first seeks assurance from Astraea that his promise to make her a star will be fulfilled (103–146). Jupiter goes to Astraea's palace, and has to bribe his way into her presence, but she agrees that his request be granted the next morning (147–252). Venus, however, is jealous, and cajoles her husband Vulcan to refuse to make any more thunderbolts should Jupiter so honour the nymph. This threat eventually causes Jupiter to forego Salmacis, though he adds to her beauty in recompense (253–360). Salmacis will not hunt with her fellow nymphs, but stays in the brook, admiring her own beauty, which is where Hermaphroditus comes upon her (361–404). There Bacchus tries to seduce her, but is prevented by Apollo, as a result of which Bacchus seeks the assistance of Mercury, who obliges by stealing the wheels of the sun's chariot (405–524). As a result, Apollo descends to ask Salmacis' help in recovering the wheels, and offers her in return a sight of the most beautiful boy ever (525–42). Salmacis obtains the chariot wheels, allowing the sun to decline and then rise again. Apollo fulfils his promise by sending Hermaphroditus to Salmacis' brook (543–624). Salmacis is immediately enamoured of Hermaphroditus, but he remains bashful and hides himself in the grass (625–734). She finds him and tries to seduce him, but when he struggles to escape she says she will go of her own accord, and hides in the grass (735–826). Supposing himself alone, Hermaphroditus strips naked to bathe in the brook, at which Salmacis does the same and embraces him (827–96). When he struggles to get away, she prays that they may never be separated. Her wish is granted, and they are united into one body, neither man nor maid (897–906). Hermaphroditus' last prayer to his parents is that whoever should bathe in the brook will be so transformed (907–22).

The Metamorphosis of Pygmalion's Image

Pygmalion disdains the love of women, until, carving an ivory statue of a beautiful, naked woman, he becomes enamoured of it (1–72). He kisses and fondles it, and eventually puts it into bed and prays to Venus to bring it to life (73–144). Then he strips naked and gets into bed with the statue, which becomes transformed into a living woman (145–92). They couple and their daughter Paphos is conceived, after whom the island of Cyprus is named (193–234).

ACKNOWLEDGEMENTS

I should like to thank David Atkinson (again) for all his help, especially in the preparation of the Glossary and Text Summaries; and, more generally, the students of Birkbeck College, who provided the impetus for this book.